WITHDRAWN

THE YALE COURSE OF HOME STUDY

BASED ON

THE CHRONICLES OF AMERICA

SUPPLEMENTARY VOLUME

THE CHRONICLES
OF AMERICA SERIES
ALLEN JOHNSON
EDITOR

GERHARD R. LOMER
CHARLES W. JEFFERYS
ASSISTANT EDITORS

THE YALE COURSE OF HOME STUDY

BASED ON
THE CHRONICLES OF AMERICA

BY RALPH H. GABRIEL
AND ARTHUR B. DARLING

NEW HAVEN: YALE UNIVERSITY PRESS
TORONTO: GLASGOW, BROOK & CO.
LONDON: HUMPHREY MILFORD
OXFORD UNIVERSITY PRESS
1924

PREFACE

This outline has been prepared for the use of the person who wishes to become familiar with the story of his country. It is intended to serve as a guide to enable him more clearly to trace the various phases in the development of the American people and to understand the relations of one phase to another. The outline may be used as a whole to study the history of the nation in its entirety or chapters may be selected to acquire a special knowledge, for example, of American foreign affairs. References are in the main to complete chapters so that the student can get the author's full thought. Page references are given in Arabic notation.

The authors are grateful to Mr. Frederick Manning for cooperation in the preparation of the chronology and to Professor Allen Johnson for a critical reading of the manuscript.

R. H. G.
A. B. D.

YALE UNIVERSITY,
NEW HAVEN, CONN.

CONTENTS

I.	A NEW WORLD	Page	1
II.	THE BEGINNINGS OF A NATION	"	7
III.	RIVALS OF THE ENGLISH FOR MASTERY OF THE CONTINENT	"	24
IV.	THE WINNING OF INDEPENDENCE	"	30
V.	OCCUPATION OF THE MISSISSIPPI VALLEY	"	37
VI.	CREATION AND INTERPRETATION OF A CONSTITUTION	"	46
VII.	PROTEST AGAINST EUROPEAN DOMINANCE	"	51
VIII.	POLITICS AND PARTISANS	"	58
IX.	THE ESTABLISHMENT OF A NEW NATIONALISM	"	65
X.	SECTIONALISM AND JACKSONIAN DEMOCRACY	"	79
XI.	COMMERCE, INDUSTRY AND THE TARIFF TO THE CIVIL WAR	"	94
XII.	THE NATIONAL BANK, FINANCE AND THE EARLY RAILROADS	"	107

CONTENTS

XIII. APPROPRIATION OF THE CONTINENT Page 114

XIV. THE RISE OF SECTIONAL STRIFE " 121

XV. THE WAR BETWEEN THE STATES " 141

XVI. THE RISE OF BIG BUSINESS " 162

XVII. THE CONSEQUENCES OF INDUS-
TRIALISM " 178

XVIII. THE NEW SECTIONALISM " 199

XIX. THE PUBLIC INTEREST PARAMOUNT " 217

XX. THE NEW RÔLE AS A WORLD POWER " 224

XXI. OUR NEIGHBORS " 245

XXII. CHRONOLOGY " 260

THE YALE COURSE OF HOME STUDY

BASED ON

THE CHRONICLES OF AMERICA

.·.

CHAPTER I

A NEW WORLD

UNKNOWN to the men of mediæval Europe two
virgin continents lay on the far side of the world.
Norse adventurers had probably touched the
northern continent at the beginning of the
Eleventh Century, but their voyages did not lead
to the spread of European settlement to the New
World. In the year 1492 an Italian dreamer sailing in the service of the rising kingdom of Spain
discovered America. But Columbus never knew
that he had come upon a vast continent whose
wide plains and tumbled mountain masses con-
cealed a fabulous wealth which was to belong to

1

future settlers from Europe, but which lay practically untouched by a primitive race that had not yet passed beyond the Stone Age.

The American Indian had made some remarkable advances toward civilization. The Iroquois in North America had developed a political organization that extended their power far and wide. The Mayas in Central America had evolved a written language and a calendar of great accuracy. They had erected buildings massive and beautiful, without the aid of beasts of burden or iron implements. It was a surprising achievement; yet the greater wonder is that the American Indians, in the midst of a wealth of natural resources which was to astound the Old World, had not accomplished more. Organized in simple tribes and tiny nations, they were totally unprepared to cope with the aggressive Europeans, throwing off the lethargy of the middle ages. They stumbled upon America while searching for better avenues to the riches of the Orient, but amazed by discovery of a New World, they remained to appropriate for themselves the birthright of the natives.

Close upon the pioneer voyages of Columbus, other explorers and conquerors penetrated the

wilderness of the Americas for the glory of Spain
and the Church, overthrew the empires of Aztecs
and Incas, and stamped the Spanish imprint upon
the southern half of the hemisphere. While
Spanish authority was spreading from Florida and
Mexico through Central and South America to
the wilds of Patagonia, other European nations
did not stand idly by. For imperial France,
Cartier laid claim to the region of the Saint Lawrence. Huguenot settlers tried to gain a foothold
in Florida. The great Champlain placed the
foundations of a New France in Acadia and
Quebec. For England, the Venetian Cabot discovered Labrador. British buccaneers, Hawkins
and Drake, harried the Spaniard on western seas,
and the great Raleigh attempted to create a
replica of Elizabethan England in the New World.
With the defeat of the Spanish Armada in 1588,
the power of the Spaniard to dispute the advances
of Englishman and Frenchman was broken. They
now faced each other in a prolonged struggle for
mastery of North America.

The Geographical Background   (The Chronicles of America)
   Climate and man   Volume 1, Chapter I
     The Norseman
   Structure of the land   "   "   II, III
   Soil and vegetation   "   "   IV

4 THE YALE COURSE OF HOME STUDY

The American Indian   Volume 1, Chapter V
    Culture and contrasts in type
        Maya, Iroquois, Eskimo, Pacific Coast Indians, and
            Indians of the Great Plains

The European Background   Volume 2, Chapter I
    Geographical ideas
    The Islands of the Atlantic
    Legends of Prester John
    Tales of Marco Polo

Discovery   "   "   II
    The early career of Columbus
      Influences upon Columbus
        Toscanelli and Behaim
        Chance voyages
        Pinzon
    The court of Ferdinand and Isabella
      Preparations for the voyage
    The voyage of 1492
      Rival Spanish and Portuguese claims   "   "   Page 78
    The fate of Columbus
      Subsequent voyages
      Death in poverty
      The name America   "   "Pages 65–66

Spanish Exploration and Colonization
    Balboa and the Pacific   1513   "   "Chapter III
    Magellan   1519
    Cortès and Mexico   1519   "   "   IV
    The conquest of Central America   "   "   V
    Pizarro in Peru   1524   "   "   VI
    The Spanish penetration of North
        America   Volume 23, Chapters I–IV
      Explorers
        Ponce de Leon, Ayllon, Narvaez, De Vaca, De Soto
          and Coronado
    Padres and settlers   Volume 23, Chapters V–X
      Florida, New Mexico, Texas, Louisiana, and
        California

French Exploration and Colonization
Cartier's voyages   Volume 4,   Chapters I–II
     The foundation of Bourbon claims
Huguenots in Florida   "   "   Pages 135–150
     Ribaut and Laudonnière
     Menendez, the sword of Spain
Champlain and New France   "   "   Chapter II
     Explorations in Acadia, 1603
     The founding of Quebec, 1608
     Champlain and the Iroquois, 1609
     Journeys into the interior
     Richelieu's colonizing company, 1629
Louis XIV and New France   "   "   IV
     The counsel of Colbert
     New France as a royal domain
     The intendants
     The sway of Frontenac   "   "   V
     Penetration of the back country   "   "   VI
         Voyageurs
         La Salle
Church and state in New France
     The priest   "   "   VII
     The seigneur   "   "   VIII
     The coureur de bois   "   "   IX
         Brandy, Indians, and furs
     The farmer and the artisan   "   "   X
     Daily life in New France   "   "   XI

English Exploration
     The voyage of John Cabot   Volume 3, Chapter I
     The rise of English sea power
         Tudor ambitions   "   "   II, III
         Rivalry with Spain and France
     The perils of Elizabeth   "   "   IV
         Catholic enmity
John Hawkins, slavers, and gentlemen
         pirates   "   "   V
     Spanish victims

English Exploration—Continued
  Sir Francis Drake, scourge of Spain
    On the Spanish Main   Volume 3, Chapter VI
    In the Pacific   "   "   VII
    In the ports of Spain   "   "   VIII
  The establishment of English sea power   "   "   IX, X
    The defeat of the Spanish Armada
    The way clear for colonization of North America
    The quest for the Northwest passage to India
  Sir Walter Raleigh and prospectors for
        England
    Gilbert, Cavendish, Frobisher
    First English settlements
      Failure
      The mystery of Virginia Dare
  The death of Drake   Volume 3, Chapter XII

CHAPTER II

WHILE Champlain and his successors were constructing a royal empire for Louis Quatorze on the Saint Lawrence, Englishmen strove to gain footholds on the Atlantic seaboard. Leaving to gentlemen adventurers the search for a sea-route to the Orient, merchants of London and Plymouth organized commercial enterprises to exploit the resources of the new world. From beginnings that they made grew the colonies that were to become the nucleus of a new nation. The quest of profit guided the establishment of Virginia and the first efforts to settle on the New England coast, but search for a religious haven led Pilgrims and Puritans to New England and Catholics to Maryland.

America, however, was not to prove a place of restful security. The vast silence of its wilderness was shattered by the tumult of strife within

the colonies. Their increasing spirit of independence roused the mother country to use a firmer hand. The early Virginians lived through the ordeals of starvation and Indian fury to establish their colony upon the economic basis of tobacco raising. Then the liberalism of their leaders ran athwart the path of King James. Their charter was revoked, and Virginia became a royal colony, the first in a succession that marked the growth of an imperial policy. The Puritans of Massachusetts came to America to set up a Bible Commonwealth in which they should live under their own religious tenets and social restrictions. Other persons could conform or go elsewhere in the wilderness. Their system, however, was immediately assailed from within. Some of the people clamored for removal of restrictions that prevented their participation in government; others resisted the control that the Puritan theocracy assumed over their consciences. Out of these dissensions were born the colonies of Rhode Island and Connecticut. Many other radicals moved northward to settle in New Hampshire and vex the soul of Gorges, Anglican and royalist proprietor. Catholic Maryland was engulfed by a tide of Puritan migration sweeping in from the

other colonies, until in self-defense Catholics were obliged to pass an "Act of Toleration" granting religious freedom to all except those who denied the divinity of Christ. Charles I became alarmed by the continuous migration of his Puritan subjects to America and determined to bring the colonies under closer royal supervision. Archbishop Laud, who had relentlessly pursued nonconformists in England, was to investigate the state of affairs in America; but the outbreak of civil war in England put a stop to the colonial plans of Charles.

Meanwhile the Dutch, emulating their stronger neighbors, had established a New Netherland on Manhattan Island and the Hudson River. Fortunate in possession of the economic center of North America, these sturdy Hollanders were rapidly establishing their own civilization about the mouth of the Hudson when war swept them into the hands of the English.

The Civil War in England, followed by the stormy rule of Cromwell, had left America to itself in all important adolescent years. After the Restoration in 1660, when Charles II resumed direction of colonial affairs, he found a dangerously independent spirit in America. His colonial sub-

jects evaded his regulations on commerce. They resented his gifts to favorites of the Carolinas, Jerseys, New York, and huge areas in Virginia as feudal domains. They disliked the governors who exercised the royal authority. New Englanders grew angry at the sight of Andros, sent to gather all the colonies from New Jersey to Maine into a Dominion of New England. It might mean greater protection against the French and Indians but it also meant the overturn of cherished Puritan institutions. A sullen watch was kept for the moment when Andros could be sent back to England and the Dominion broken up. The opportunity came in 1688 with the overthrow of James II in England. Already in Virginia, Bacon's rebellion against the rule of the royal governor, Berkeley, had burst into flames, revealing the stark outlines of the approaching American Revolution.

During the Eighteenth Century the American colonies continued on their course of evading the imperial restriction on commerce and harassing the royal governors who attempted to execute the will of the Crown. They were establishing habits of community life and social customs peculiar to their own localities, whether Puritan in New England, Quaker in Pennsylvania, or Cavalier in

Virginia. But they were facing a danger in common with the mother country, the menace of the French in the back country, a danger which held them close, in spite of diverging interests.

English Colonization
  Virginia and the southern colonies
    Commercial enterprise in Virginia   Volume 5, Chapter **I**
      The London and Plymouth companies
        The land grant
        Government
      The adventurers and the land   "   "   **II**
      Jamestown   "   "   **III**
      Misery and adventure   "   "   **IV, V**
        Captain John Smith
        "The Sea Venture"
        "Starving Time"
        The Arrival of Delaware
      The vigorous rule of Dale   "   "   **VI**
        The charter of 1612
        Rolfe and tobacco
        Argall and the French in Maine
        The menace of Spain
      Sandys and the liberal government   "   "   **VII**
        Yeardley, governor, 1619
        The House of Burgesses
        Cargoes of slaves and women
        The Indian massacre, 1622
      The displeasure of King James   "   "   **VIII**
        The first royal province
    Maryland, refuge of Roman Catholics   "   "   **IX**
      Calvert, favorite of the King
        Land grant — Newfoundland
                   Virginia
      Feudal domain
    Settlement, 1634
      Peace with the Indians

English Colonization—Continued
  The hostility of Virginia
   William Claiborne and Kent Island
  Democratic stirrings   Volume 5, Pages 140–147
   The Act of Toleration, 1649
The reign of Berkeley in Virginia   " "   Chapter X
 Puritans, Papists, and Anglicans
 The Indian fury
 The effect of the Commonwealth on
  Virginia   " "   XI
  The coming of the Cavaliers
   The "Old Dominion"
  The retirement of Berkeley
   Submission to the Commonwealth
  Claiborne's attack on Maryland
 The effect of the Restoration in Virginia
  Grants to favorites of Charles II
  The return of Berkeley
  Navigation Acts   Volume 5, Pages 245–247
   England's trade policy
 Nathaniel Bacon, first American
  revolutionist   " "   Chapter XII
  Berkeley's tyranny
   Local government
  The Indian uprising
   Suppression by Bacon   " "   XIII
  Larger plans
   Berkeley's rage
  The rebellion
Eighteenth century Virginia   " "   XV
 The Shenandoah
Maryland after the Restoration   " " Pages 190–198
 Proprietary control
 The decline of Catholic freedom
 Eighteenth century Maryland
The Carolinas   " "   Chapter XIV
 The proprietors, 1663
 Early settlements
  Albemarle, Virginian back-country

English Colonization—Continued
  Cape Fear, Barbadians
  Charleston, colonists from England
  Locke's "Fundamental Constitutions"
  Rejection by the frontiersmen
  Pirates, heretics, radicals from Europe, and restless
   Virginians
 The founding of Georgia, 1733 Volume 5, Chapter XV
  Oglethorpe, philanthropist
   English debtors
   European refugees
  The wall against Spanish Florida
Plymouth and the New England colonies
 The exodus of the Pilgrims   Volume 6, Chapter I
 Changes in England
  The pressure of religion
  The men of Scrooby
  Sojourn in Holland
 Settlement in America
  The Mayflower Compact
  The place of the Plymouth colony in American
   history
 Puritans on Massachusetts Bay Volume 6, Chapter II
 Forerunners: Weston, Blackstone, Maverick
  Endicott at Salem
 John Winthrop and the Cambridge Agreement
  The removal of the company to America
  The Great Migration of 1630
 The erection of a Bible Commonwealth
  Expulsion of malcontents
   Anne Hutchinson
   Roger Williams
The expansion of New England Volume 6, Chapter III
 New colonies from old
  Rhode Island and Roger Williams
   The arrival of the Hutchinsonians
   William Coddington
   The appearance of Gorton, free-thinker
   The Patent of 1643

English Colonization—Continued

        The Charter of 1663   Volume 6, Pages 113–114

   Connecticut
     The Dutch on the Connecticut river
     Saybrook
     Thomas Hooker's migration to Hartford
     "Fundamental Orders"
     The New Haven colony
       Ultra Puritans
   New Hampshire
     Grants of Mason and Gorges
       Dover
       Portsmouth
     Exiles from Massachusetts
       Exeter
       Hampton
     The conflict of titles, grants, and claims
       Anglican versus Puritan
       Proprietors versus Settlers
 Town life and intercolonial affairs
  The people and their customs   Volume 6, Chapter IV
   Common beliefs
     Science, witchcraft, and medicine
     Local government
     The daily routine
   Common cause
     The New England Confederation
     Enemies of Englishmen
       The Dutch
       The Indians   Volume 6, Chapter VIII
         The Pequot War
         King Philip
The effect of the Restoration in New England
  Intercolonial rivalries   Volume 6, Chaper VI
   The favor of Charles II
     The confirmation of charters
   The success of Connecticut
     The absorption of New Haven
     The consolidation of Rhode Island

English Colonization—Continued
       The reassurance of Massachusetts
     The policy of the Merry Monarch
      Conciliation
      Closer control   Volume 6, Page 102
        The navigation system
               Compare Volume 5, Pages 245–247
   Colonial restiveness   Volume 6, Chapter VII
    Wayward Massachusetts
    The role of Maverick
    The royal commission of investigation, 1664
      A cold reception
   The special mission of Randolph   Volume 6, Chapter IX
    The royal displeasure
    Discipline for Massachusetts
      The revocation of the charter, 1684
   The Dominion of New England   Volume 6, Chapter X
    Governor Andros
    The menace of New France
    The union of the New England colonies
      The resistance of the colonies
   The effect of the Revolution of 1688
    The overthrow of Andros
   The new charter for Massachusetts Volume 6, Chapter XI
    The end of colonial isolation

Although the Puritans left England to find political and religious seclusion in America, they did not desire to break off commercial intercourse with the outside world. Their ships were soon competing with English and Dutch merchantmen for traffic among the lands that bordered the Atlantic Ocean.

   Puritan seafarers   Volume 36, Chapter I
    The coastwise trade with Virginia
    Negroes and rum
    Treasure hunting
      Sir William Phips
  The Middle Colonies
   The foothold of Holland in America   Volume 7, Chapter I
    Henry Hudson, 1609
    The Dutch West India Company   "   "   II

16 THE YALE COURSE OF HOME STUDY

English Colonization—Continued

      First settlements, 1623

      The fur trade

    Patroons and tenants   Volume 7, Chapter III

      A feudal land system

    Dutch colonial management   "   "   IV

      Minuit and Manhattan

      Van Twiller and Hartford

        English encroachment

      Kieft and the Indians

      Stuyvesant and the settlers

        Van der Donck

        The English on Long Island

        The treaty of Hartford, 1650

      The arrival of the English fleet, 1664

    Dutch classes and customs   Volume 7, Chapters V, VI

      Preachers and teachers

      Burghers and farmers

    Neighbors of the Dutch   "   "   VII

      The Indians

      The Swedes on the Delaware

      The English in New England

New York under the rule of England "   "   VIII

      The surprise attack

      The Duke's laws

      The Dutch reconquest

      Governors Andros and Dongan

      The Leisler rebellion   "   "   IX

      William and Mary

    Eighteenth century life

      The home port of pirates   "   "   X

        Captain Kidd   Compare Volume 36, Chapter I

      The menace of the slaves   Volume 7, Chapter XIII

The founding of Pennsylvania

    Mystics and business men

      William Penn, Quaker   Volume 8, Chapter I

        Land for royal debts

      His feudal domain   "   "   II

      Philadelphia   "   "   III

English Colonization—Continued

The English and Germans in
    Pennsylvania   Volume 8, Chapter IV
Problems of the proprietors   "   "   V
Relations with the Indians   "   "   VI
Quaker government in the eigh-
    teenth century   "   "   VII
The Jerseys, royal gifts
Lords Berkeley and Carteret   "   "   VIII
    Puritan settlers
    Quaker interests
    Rival colonial authorities
Landed aristocrats   "   "   IX
Contending religious sects   "   "   X
The union of the Jerseys   "   "   XI
    Royal province, 1702
    Proprietary quitrents
    Princeton University
Delaware, independent colony   "   "   XII
    Settlers — English, Dutch, Swedes
The rule of Penn   "   "   XIII
    Home rule, 1703

British Imperial Policy and Navigation Acts

The significance of civil war in England
    Charles I and Laud's commission   Volume 6, Pages 27–35
    The Long Parliament
    Earl of Warwick, governor of the Colonies, 1643
    The Navigation Ordinance, 1651
                            Volume 5, Pages 156, 245
The Restoration in England
The establishment of a colonial commercial system
                            Volume 5, Pages 245–247
    The navigation acts   Volume 6, Page 102
    Charles II
        Act of 1660
            British vessels
        Act of 1663
            British ports

British Imperial Policy and Navigation Acts—Continued
> Act of 1673
>> Enumerated goods
> King William
>> Act of 1696
>>> Administration
>>> Admiralty courts
The plan for colonial administration and defence

The Dominion of New England Volume 6, Pages 177–193
Volume 7, Pages 149–151
Volume 8, Pages 177–179

Partly by chance the British Crown in its consent to the establishment of colonies in America allowed three types to grow up. In some cases individuals like William Penn or groups of favorites like the Carolina proprietors were granted large domains over which the grantees exercised feudal control. This was the proprietary province. The communities of Rhode Island and Connecticut, which had developed without original grants from the Crown, sought and secured charters of incorporation which gave the people of the two colonies powers to elect their own governors and direct their own affairs within specified limits. This was the corporate colony. When James I revoked the charter of Virginia and made it into a royal province, he established the third type of colony. Thereafter Virginia was a part of the imperial domain and the governor was appointed directly by the Crown. When the British realized that they had an empire in America and, further, that the colonies were getting out of hand, they turned more and more to the royal type of colony as the best way to govern the empire and hold its component parts close to the mother country. They, accordingly, began the policy of eliminating wherever possible the other two types of colonies.

The trend toward royal provinces

Virginia, 1625	Volume 5, Pages 103–110
New York, 1685	Volume 7, Pages 148–150
Massachusetts and Maine, 1691	Volume 6, Chapter IX–XI
New Hampshire, 1691	Volume 6, Page 197
Maryland, 1691 (restored in 1715)	
	Volume 5, Pages 190–198

British Imperial Policy and Navigation Acts—Continued

New Jersey, 1702 — Volume 8, Chapter XI

North Carolina ⎱
South Carolina ⎰ 1719–1729 — Volume 5, Page 235

Georgia, 1754

Pennsylvania — Volume 8, Pages 118–124

Rhode Island ⎱
Connecticut ⎰ — Volume 6, Pages 192–193

The imperial organization of Great Britain and its colonies gave to the mother country an authority superior to colonial governments in different respects. The Crown had one veto over colonial actions, exercised upon advice of the imperial board of trade. It had another in the power of the royal governor in the colony to refuse approval of the acts of colonial assemblies. The judiciary of Great Britain had the right of judicial review and annulment of the decisions of colonial courts. Acts of Parliament, as the imperial legislature, took precedence over acts of colonial legislatures where they conflicted, and Parliament under the imperial theory could legislate for any part as well as the whole of the British Empire. Finally, colonial acts could be rendered without effect by royal disallowance without the formality of a veto.

Colonial governments and imperial authority

The Crown, Judiciary, and Parliament

Typical cases

Virginia — Volume 5, Pages 103–111

Massachusetts — Volume 6, Pages 185–189

New Jersey — Volume 8, Pages 180–185

Pennsylvania — Volume 8, Pages 118–124

Imperial regulation and control

Royal governor and colonial
assembly in New York — Volume 7, Chapter XI

A typical example

Acts of Parliament

Restraint of colonial manufactures

The Molasses Act, 1733 — Volume 11, Pages 26–27

Personal liberty

Freedom of the press — Volume 7, Chapter XII

British Imperial Policy and Navigation Acts—Continued
    First steps toward colonial union
        The New England Confederation, 1642
                           Volume 6, Pages 88–99
        The Dominion of New England, 1688
                         Volume 6, Pages 177–193
                         Volume 7, Pages 149–151
                         Volume 8, Pages 88–89
      The Congress at New York, 1690   Volume 7, Page 157
      The Albany Congress, 1754   Volume 7, Pages 219–221
                         Volume 10, Pages 159–160
                         Volume 8, Pages 88-89

Life in the English Colonies
    Settlers and their homes   Volume 9, Chapter I
      Nova Scotia to Georgia
      Sea coast and back country
      Englishman and "foreigner"
        Huguenot
        German
        Ulsterman
    Town and country   "   "   II
      Freeholders and tenants
      New England towns and Virginian counties
        The middle region, a fusion of both
      Southern plantations
        A landed aristocracy
    Colonial houses   Volume 9, Chapter III
      The streets of Boston
      Dutch houses in New York
      Quaker dwellings in Philadelphia
                 Compare Volume 8, Chapter III
      The homes of Charleston
      Country dwellings
        New England farmhouses
        The Southern planter's home
    Colonial dress and family life   Volume 9, Chapter IV
      Rich and poor
      Master and laborer

Life in the English Colonies—Continued
  Townsman and farmer
  Importations from England
  Adornments and personal care
  Colonial marriages
    Early betrothals
    Few divorces
  Family affairs
    The training of children
    Sickness and death
    Funerals
Necessities and recreations   Volume 9, Chapter V
  Provisions
    Transportation
    Perishable foods
    Hunting and fishing
    Garden truck
    Spices, coffee, lemons
  Drinking and smoking
    The tavern
      Business, news, politics
  Games and sports
    Cards, gambling, horse-racing, and fairs
  Assemblies, music, and drama
Intellectual culture   Volume 9, Chapter VI
  Schools
    The New England system   Volume 33, Chapter I
    Maryland Free School Act, 1694—   Volume 9, Page 132
    Quaker and German education   Volume 33, Chapter III
      Religious direction
    Dutch parochial schools   Volume 33, Chapter II
    Private tutors in the South
      Education of wealthy youths in England
    Limited opportunities for girls
  Christian teaching for Indians and negroes
Higher education   Volume 33, Chapter IV
      Harvard, William and Mary, Yale, Princeton,
      Rhode Island (Brown), Dartmouth, King's
      College (Columbia), University of Pennsylvania

Life in the English Colonies—Continued
>> Professional training
>> Medicine, law, art
>> Study in Europe
> The use of languages and variety of reading
>> Notable collections of books
>> The colonial bookseller
Religious life   Volume 9, Chapter VII
> Sectarian divisions
> The minister in New England
> The Anglican rector in the South
> Backsliders and wayward clergy
> Music in church services
Labor in colonial times   "   "   VIII
> The farmhand
> The skilled artisan
> Indentured servants
>> "Soul drivers"
>> Contracted immigrants
> Apprentices
> Transported convicts
> Negro slaves
>> The African slave trade
>> Slave markets
>>> Newport, R. I.
>>> Charleston, S. C.
>> Domestic and field slaves
>> Master and slave woman
Travel   "   "   IX
> Voyages to England, the Continent, and the West Indies
> Intercolonial travel
>> Northern summer resorts
>> European observers
> Routes
>> By water and land
>>> Horseback and coach
A survey of sectional differences   Volume 9, Pages 230–237

The Literature of the Colonial Period
  The restless spirit of America   Volume 34, Chapter I
    The English tradition
    The stir of the frontier
  The first men of letters   "   "   II
    Capt. John Smith and William Strachey
    Bradford and Winthrop
  The clergy
    Hooker and Cotton
  The younger generation   "   "   III
    The contrast between Cotton Mather and Samuel
      Sewall
    Jonathan Edwards, philosopher

The Greatest Colonial Figure
  Benjamin Franklin
    Man of letters   Volume 34, Chapter III
    Educator   Volume 33, Chapter V
    Scientist   Volume 37, Chapter I
    Statesman
      Advocate of colonial union   Volume 7, Page 220
                           Volume 10, Page 160
                           Volume 13, Page 50
      Citizen of Pennsylvania   Volume 8, Pages 56–124
      Colonial agent at London   Volume 11, Chapter I
      Revolutionist
        Member of Congress   Volume 12, Pages 50, 93
        Minister to France   Volume 13, Chapter I
        Negotiator of peace
      A framer of the Constitution   Pages 113, 134

CHAPTER III

ALTHOUGH Spain lost control of the high seas with
the defeat of the Armada, Spanish authority still
remained dominant in Central and South America,
and Spanish settlements in the southern part of
North America increased steadily until they extended from Florida around the gulf coast to
Mexico and up the Pacific coast far into California. It was not from the Spaniard, however,
busily engaged as he was in exploiting an empire
in his own way, that the Englishman on the Atlantic coast was to meet strong opposition. Except
on the frontier of the Floridas, they nowhere came
in contact. It was from the Frenchman to the
north and west, who was penetrating the back
country in search of furs, fortifying the strategic
points, and establishing an inland empire, lightly
but firmly held. The New Englander was in con-

tact with the French inhabitant of Quebec and
Acadia. The frontiersman of New York, Pennsylvania, or Virginia came frequently upon the
French trader at the very back door of his own
colony.

Even if there had been no European or Oriental
quarrels to set their mother countries upon each
other, the colonials would sooner or later have
come to blows. The French in Acadia menaced
the growing commerce of New England, and the
Puritan hated Popish neighbors. The specter of
an Indian warrior infuriated by French brandy and
religious bigotry was ever in the mind of the
English backwoodsman. The French feared the
advance of the English pioneer over the mountains
into the rich Ohio valley threatening the fur trade
upon which his colonial empire was based. These
antagonisms were stirred to violence by unending
quarrels in Europe. The feud between England
and France was fought out in a series of wars,
named by the English colonials: King William's
War, 1689–1697, Queen Anne's War, 1702–1713,
King George's War, 1739–1748, and The French
and Indian War, 1754–1763. In all the plan was
the same. Englishmen launched successive attacks against Quebec and Montreal and strove to

win and hold Acadia. Frenchmen harassed the
frontier with fire and Indian vengeance, countered
the English blows, and clung desperately to the
Ohio valley. In the end, the English captured
Quebec and Montreal and forced the French to
deliver up their inland empire. For allying themselves with the French against the English, the
Spaniards were given in 1763 Louisiana—all that
France had claimed west of the Mississippi south
of the great unexplored regions to the northwest.
The triumph of England, however, brought with
peace a new menace to the British Empire. The
colonial inhabitants of the seaboard colonies
watched the French peril vanish with mixed emotions. They exulted in victory, for the last war
had been in a larger sense their war with the
French and the Indians. The French were gone.
For the Indians they had only contempt. With a
new feeling of security and power, they faced the
settlement of their relations with the Imperial
British Government.

The Spaniards to the South and West   Volume 23, Chapter V
   Florida   Volume 5, Pages 33–36, 88–89, 206, 232
   New Mexico   Volume 23, Chapter VI
   Texas   "   "   VIII
   Louisiana   "   "   IX
     Spain in the French and Indian War Volume 19, Chapter IV
   California   Volume 23, Chapters VII, X

The French on the North and West
  Early Virginian hostility to the French in Maine
                                  Volume 5, Pages 87–88
    French pioneers in the West   Volume 10, Chapter V
      New Orleans
      Search for the Western Sea
      English competitors from Hudson Bay
      The clash in the valley of the Ohio   "   "   VI

The Feud between England and France
  "King William's War" 1689–1697   "   "   I
    Frontenac and Phips
      Schenectady
      Phips at Port Royal in Acadia
      Phips before Quebec
        Failure
      Schuyler's expedition into Canada
      The advance of Frontenac in 1696
      The peace of Ryswick
  The contrast of French and English
    colonies   "   "   II
    European rivalry and colonial strife
    Catholic and Protestant
    French despotism and English self-government
    The difference of population
  "Queen Anne's War" 1702–1713   Volume 10, Chapter III
    French aggression on the frontier of New England
      Deerfield massacre 1704
    The march of Nicholson against Port Royal
    The expedition of Hill and Walker against Quebec
      Dismal failure
    The treaty of Utrecht
  The French entrenchment at Louisburg Volume 10, Chapter IV
    Thirty years of peace
    Walpole's policy
  "King George's War" 1739–1748
    The attack of New England on Louisburg
      The victory of Pepperell

The Feud between England and France—Continued
    The peace of Aix-la-Chapelle
      The return of Louisburg to the French
      The anger of Massachusetts
  "The French and Indian War" 1754–1763
                         Volume 10, Pages 151–163
    Rival claims to the Ohio Valley   Volume 8, Chapter VI
      The French at Fort Le Bœuf   Volume 18, Pages 75–83
        The mission of George Washington
      The English at Pittsburgh
        Fort Duquesne
        Washington's defeat of Jumonville
        The battle of Great Meadows
      Colonial preparations for defence
        The Albany Congress 1754
    The campaigns of 1755
      Braddock's disaster
      Johnson's expedition against Crown Point
        The victory on Lake George   Volume 7, Chapter XIV
      Expulsion of the Acadians   Volume 10, Chapter VII
        Allegiance to England or deportation
  Montcalm in Canada   Volume 10, Chapter VIII
      The jealousy of Vaudreuil
      Montcalm's thrust into New York
        Oswego
        Lake Champlain, 1757
        Defeat of Abercrombie at Ticonderoga, 1758
        Obstacles at Quebec and
          Versailles   Volume 10, Chapter IX
    William Pitt, war minister   "   "   X
      The capture of Louisburg
      The capture of Duquesne   "   "   Page 198
        Pittsburgh
      The English campaign of 1759
        Wolfe before Quebec
          The Plains of Abraham
        The march of Amherst on Montreal
    Indian friends of the French in the
      Southwest   Volume 18, Pages 83–87

The Feud between England and France—Continued
The fall of Canada   Volume 10, Chapter XI
The convergence of three British armies on
Montreal, 1760
Amherst, commander-in-chief
The capture of Montreal
The peace of Paris, 1763
Indian resistance to English control
Pontiac's conspiracy   Volume 19, Chapter I

CHAPTER IV

THE WINNING OF INDEPENDENCE

Victory in 1763 over France in the war for world dominion gave to Great Britain, besides an extended control over India, practically the whole of the North American continent east of the Mississippi river. The British Empire had suddenly more than doubled in area. With title to the land came the duty of administration and protection. The Imperial government was obliged to reorganize the commercial system, to find new revenues, and at the same time to consolidate its conquests. Long since grown accustomed to handle their own affairs rather as they willed, the Americans resented the unexpected attempt to establish more effective imperial regulation of their economic life and control over their political affairs. In successive ministries, Grenville, Rockingham, Townshend, and North all tried to build up a colonial policy that would reconcile the needs of

the empire with the wishes of the colonists. The struggles over this problem precipitated the Revolution.

Out of the bitterness of the first year of bloodshed grew a strong demand for independence. The Declaration of July 4, 1776, proclaimed that the British colonies from New Hampshire to Georgia had broken the ancient ties that bound them to the homeland and had set out for themselves as the United States of America. Seven years of war, however, were required before Great Britain would accept this assertion as a fact.

The contest was manifold in character. It was both a rebellion against imperial control and a feud at home between patriots and loyalists, the tragedy of which was heightened by the frightfulness of Indian raids and the grim retaliation of frontiersmen. Following Burgoyne's surrender at Saratoga, France came openly to the assistance of the revolutionary states, to get vengeance on the old enemy of the Fleur-de-Lys. Spain and Holland joined France. A conflict that started as an insurrection about Boston became a world war.

Although the French alliance virtually made certain the ultimate outcome, the Revolution was

greatly aided by the incompetence of Britain's generals. On three occasions, at the battle of Long Island, at Morristown during the critical year of 1776, and at Valley Forge in 1777, General Howe failed to seize his opportunity to destroy the small army of Washington and remove this bulwark of the American cause from the field. The will of Washington and the devotion of the small group about him were in large measure responsible for bringing the American Revolution through the years of discouragement to success. Unable to disperse the American army and to prevent a coalition of European enemies, Great Britain grew tired of a prolonged and expensive war across three thousand miles of sea, acknowledged the independence of her old colonies, and met their terms for peace.

The British Empire in 1763   Volume 11, Chapters I, II
   Territorial acquisitions
   The Proclamation of 1763

Grenville's Imperial Policy
   The colonial agent in England
   The British office-holder in America
   The Revenue Act of 1764
   The Quartering Act
   The Stamp Act

American Resistance   "   "   III
   The Stamp Act Congress
   Sons of Liberty

The Rockingham Repeal   Volume 11, Chapter **IV**
    The Amendment of Revenue Act   "   "   Page 114
    The Declaratory Act

Townshend's Change of the Imperial
      Policy   "   "   Chapter **IV**
    The Townshend Acts
    The Liberty
    Troops in Boston
    Non-importation agreements
    The Boston Massacre

The Influence of Lord North
    The repeal of Townshend duties except that on tea
    The Royal reaction

The Agitation by Samuel Adams   Volume 11, Chapter **V**
    His use of the caucus   Volume 43, Page 20
    The publication of Governor Hutchinson's letters
    The East India Regulating Act   Volume 11, Chapter **VI**
      The tea parties
      North's punitive acts

The First Continental Congress   "   "   **VI**
    American philosophy
    Collective action
      The Declaration of Rights
      The Association
    The party of opposition   "   "   Page 231
      Loyalists

The Outbreak of War   "   "   Chapter **VI**
    North and Burke on conciliation
    Lexington and Concord
    The Second Continental Congress
      Washington, commander-in-chief   Volume 12, Chapter **I**
      Dickinson's petition to the King

34 THE YALE COURSE OF HOME STUDY

Growing Sentiment for Independence   Volume 11, Pages 245–250
  British methods of suppression
  Paine's "Common Sense"   Volume 12, Chapter III
  The Declaration

Early Campaigns of the War
  Washington in New England   "   "   II
    Ticonderoga
    The invasion of Canada
    The siege of Boston
  The British campaign of 1776   "   "   IV
    The repulse at Fort Moultrie
    Lake Champlain   "   "   Page 53
    The capture of New York   "   "   Chapter IV
    The march into New Jersey
    Washington's brilliant counter offensive
      The battle of Trenton
      Winter at Morristown
        Howe's failure
  The British plan for 1777   "   "   V
    Burgoyne and St. Leger from Canada   "   "   VI
    Surrender at Saratoga
    Howe to Philadelphia   "   "   V
    The Loyalists
    Winter at Valley Forge   "   "   VII
      Intrigues against Washington
      Howe's failure

The American Alliance with France   "   "   VIII
  Franklin
  North's peace proposals   "   "   Page 190
  French aid   "   "   Chapter X

Operations from 1778 to 1781
  The evacuation of Philadelphia   "   "   Page 196
    Monmouth
  Newport   "   "   Page 201
  John Paul Jones and the American
    Navy   "   "   Page 205

Operations from 1778 to 1781—Continued
  The Privateers of '76   Volume 36, Chapters II, III
    Their training
      The fishing fleet of Massachusetts
      The whalers of Nantucket
    Raids upon British commerce
    Captures of British seamen
    Notable commanders
      Haraden
      Talbot
      Geddes
    The fate of Nantucket
  The British campaign in the South   Volume 12, Chapter IX
  Tory raids
  The Franco-American siege of Yorktown "   "   XI
    The surrender of Cornwallis

The Formation of the Confederation   Volume 13, Chapter III
  Revolutionary state constitutions   Pages 40–43
  The Articles   Pages 52–54;175–189

The Treaty of Peace
  The change in British ministry   Volume 12, Page 268
  The preliminary treaty with Great
    Britain   Pages 272–276
  The formal treaty of Versailles   Volume 13, Chapter I

The Evacuation of New York   Volume 12, Chapter XI
The Departure of the Loyalists

The Literature of the Revolution   Volume 34, Chapter IV
  The spirit of daring
    Loyalist pleaders for repose
    Letters from an American Farmer
    The poet — Freneau
    Writers of prose and orators
      James Otis and Patrick Henry
      Samuel Adams
      John Adams

The Literature of the Revolution—Continued
    Thomas Paine
    Alexander Hamilton
    Thomas Jefferson
      The Declaration of Independence

CHAPTER V

LONG before the Revolution restless individuals moved up the eastern slopes of the Appalachian mountains and penetrated the upland valleys. They had pushed farther and farther away from the seaboard and, as the wilderness had closed about them, had lost all feeling of dependence upon the mother country. The authority of the King was but a shadow; self sufficient backwoodsmen began to forget or ignore His Majesty's government. Many pioneers of English stock moved into this back country but more numerous were immigrants from North Ireland, Scotch in blood and Presbyterian in religion. With them, but maintaining their own identity, came groups of Scotch Highlanders and Germans from the Rhineland whose recent stay in the valleys of Pennsylvania had fastened upon them the name, "Pennsylvania Dutch." Following close upon the path-

finders and traders these peoples moved coura-
geously into the forest and the mountains to settle
in little log cabin communities, chopping away
the woods to get farms and fighting savagely with
the Indians to hold what they had taken.

In eastern Tennessee the settlers on the Watauga river bound themselves together under
simple regulations of government. When Ferguson and his Tories invaded the back country,
the men of Watauga caught the spirit of the Revolution that had swept the seaboard since 1775.
They hurried through the mountain passes to cut
off Ferguson's raiders and destroyed them in the
fierce fight at King's Mountain. Thrilled by the
thought of independence, these "overhill" people
set up a new state of Franklin and sought admission to the Confederation. But North Carolina
had claims that could not be overlooked by the
Congress of the Confederation and the State of
Franklin sank back into dependence upon the
older commonwealth. When the uncertain days
of the Confederation had passed and the United
States of America had taken form under the
Constitution, it was included in the new state of
Tennessee.

Meanwhile Daniel Boone had led the way into

the "dark and bloody ground" of Kentucky. In that no man's land his successors held on, in spite of the constant ravages of Indian war parties, until their little settlements grew into the new state of Kentucky, the first of those west of the Alleghanies to be admitted to the Union. Far out to the west in Tennessee, James Robertson led a pioneer band to settle on the Cumberland river, the beginning of Nashville. There, as an outpost, these pioneers held their ground against the Indians and in defiance of British intrigues and Spanish alarm.

North of the Ohio river the American pioneer with equal determination was defying the wishes of the mother country to regulate the settlement of the Indian country. British ministers might declare that the region between the Alleghanies and the Mississippi was closed to settlers from the seaboard colonies, but the frontiersman did not abandon his rude cabin and the clearing that he had made in the forest beside some tributary of the Ohio river. The revolt of the seaboard colonies multiplied the hardships of the frontier. More Indian war parties, incited now by British officers in the frontier forts, terrorized the settlements with tomahawk and torch. The frontiersmen

struck back with equal savagery. George Rogers Clark saw the opportunity to break the power of the British in the Northwest, and in the name of Virginia led a band of frontiersmen on an expedition to the Illinois region where he surprised the English garrisons and forced the British to retire upon Detroit.

When the war was over, the victorious colonies found themselves possessed of an empire stretching from the Alleghanies to the Mississippi. Already the several states had abandoned their sovereign claims and had avoided all disputes of ownership by giving the whole territory to the Confederation to be held as a national domain. In 1787, the Congress of the Confederation passed the famous Northwest Ordinance which provided for the organization of the region north of the Ohio, and which laid the foundations for the subsequent territorial policy of the United States. There remained the task of pushing back the Indian, of establishing settlements, allotting the lands, and organizing local governments. The story is all too frequently one of sordidness and greed but from first to last it is a tale of daring and relentless determination. The Indian fought doggedly to hold back the flood of whites, but from the start

his cause was lost. Tecumseh in desperation sought to unite all the tribes against the common foe and then turned to an open alliance with the British in Canada. But his people were not ready for such a union. At Tippecanoe and the Thames his hopes perished and in the latter battle the great chieftain gave up his life.

Meanwhile the never ending stream of home-seekers poured down the Ohio and spread out on the rich lands to the south, west, and north. The Indian was swept on, first, into the far northwest and, then, beyond the Mississippi. In this flood of pioneers were Connecticut Yankees, Pennsylvanian farmers, Virginians, and Carolinians. They came in their Conestoga wagons or on Ohio flat boats, the thrifty mingling with the thriftless, those who looked forward to success with those who looked back upon failure, American born and foreign born. Poured into the life of the frontier these clashing types retained some of their original characteristics. But common handicaps and dangers forced them into the same hard mold of backwoods life. They merged into a new figure, the Westerner.

Washington's Vision of the West   Volume 21, Chapter I
The First Immigrants: Non-English stock   Volume 35, Chapter I

The Old Back Country
 The Shenandoah and Yadkin valleys   Volume 18, Chapter I
  Ulstermen and Highlanders
  The trek of the Pennsylvania Dutch
 Frontier folkways   "   "   II

Trails and Roads across the Mountains   Volume 21, Chapter II
 The pathfinders   Volume 18, Chapter III
  Trade with the Indians
  McGillivray and Adair
  The wanderings of Daniel Boone   "   "   V
  Florida
  Kentucky

Watauga — Eastern Tennessee   "   "   VIII
 Relation to the Regulation movement
 Adventurous spirits
  James Robertson
  John Sevier
 The Association
 War with the Indians
 "Bonnie Kate Sherill"
 The back-country men at King's
  Mountain   "   "   IX
 The thrill of independence
  The State of Franklin   "   "   X

Kentucky
 The battle ground of the Indians
  Daniel Boone   "   "   VI
 Settlers on the "Dark and Bloody
  Ground"   "   "   VII
  Henderson and Harrod

Western Tennessee
 The advance of Robertson   "   Pages 184–194
 British intrigues with the Indians   "   Chapter X
  Spanish alarms

Western Tennessee—Continued
> Alexander McGillivray, Creek
>> chieftain   Volume 14, Pages 83–87
> James Wilkinson, traitor

The Inveterate Pioneer
> The migration of Daniel Boone to the
>> Missouri   Volume 18, Chapter XI

The Fight for the Northwest
> The Indian rejection of the English conquest of Canada
>> Pontiac's conspiracy   Volume 19, Chapter I
> Forbidden land
>> The Proclamation of 1763   "   "   II
>> The Quebec Act   "   "   III
> The Revolution in the Northwest
>> Indian raids
>>> English supplies
>> George Rogers Clark, conqueror of the Illinois country
>> The British counter advance   Volume 19, Chapter IV
>>> Clark's victory at Vincennes
>> The Spanish demonstration from St. Louis against
>>> the British in Michigan

The Ordinance of 1787
> The foundation of a colonial system   Volume 19, Chapter V
> The genesis of the Ordinance   Volume 13, Chapter IV
>> The cession of western lands by the several states
>> The Ordinance of 1784
>> The lobby of the Ohio company
> Progressive treaties with the Indians
>> Disregard of Indian rights by the white settlers

Ohio   Volume 19, Chapter V
> Speculation and immigration
>> War veterans and western lands
>> The Ohio Company
>> Rev. Manasseh Cutler
>>> Man of God and lobbyist

Ohio—Continued
  The founding of Marietta, 1788
    The residence of Gov. St. Clair
  The Symmes grant
    The birth of Cincinnati
      The capital of the Northwest Territory, 1790
  The Indian menace
    Savage vengeance   Volume 14, Pages 93–103
      British encouragement
      The defeat of St. Clair, 1791
    The success of Wayne
      The battle of Fallen Timbers, 1794
        The defeat of the Indians under the British
          guns of Fort Miami
        The Indian treaties of 1795
          Fifteen years of peace
  Development of transportation
    Rivers   Volume 21, Chapter III
    Wagon roads   "   "   IV

The settlement of the Northwest   Volume 19, Chapter VI
  The stream of homeseekers down the Ohio from
      Pittsburgh
    Alarm in the depleted eastern states
    The flat boat trade   Volume 21, Chapter V
  The Western Reserve   Volume 19, Chapter VI
    New Connecticut
  The Seven Ranges
    Pennsylvanians
  The Scioto Valley
    Virginians
  The frontier melting pot
    The clash of types
    Common handicaps and dangers
    The birth of common customs   "   "   VII
      The schooling of the woodsman
      Log-rolling and house-raising
      Camp meetings

The settlement of the Northwest—Continued
The Northwest as seen by foreign
    travelers   Volume 21, Chapter VI
The division of the territory
    Ohio and Indiana   Volume 19, Pages 131–132

The banishment of the Indian
Tecumseh, leader of a lost cause   "   Chapter VIII
    The expansion of the white population in Indiana
        Settlers from Kentucky
        Trespass upon Indian lands
           Destruction of their hunting grounds
        The white man's contempt
           The degradation of the Indian
    Ineffectual Congressional legislation
    The wrath of the Indian
        Tecumseh, successor of Pontiac
           The plan for an Indian confederation
           The Prophet's town
        The alarm of the white man
           The conference of Gov. Harrison and Tecumseh
               The land cessions of 1809
    The approach of war
        Tecumseh's mission to the Southern Indians
        The advance of Harrison
           The battle of Tippecanoe, 1811
    Tecumseh's alliance with the British
      in the War of 1812   Volume 19, Pages 151–160
                     Compare Volume 17, Chapter II
The effect on the Northwest of the
    British defeat   Volume 19, Chapter IX
    The rush of westward migration
    The penetration of the Upper Mississippi Valley   "   XI
        Pike's expedition, 1805
        Rivalry with the British for the Indian trade
        The discovery of lead ore
    The last stand of the Indian in the Old Northwest
        Black Hawk's War, 1830–1832

CHAPTER VI

CREATION AND INTERPRETATION OF A CONSTITUTION

THE Second Continental Congress, summoned to remonstrate with the home government, remained at Philadelphia and became the *de facto* Revolutionary government. But the colonies that had thrown off British rule and established state governments under written constitutions recognized the Continental Congress only as a central agency which under force of necessity assumed authority in a common cause. The states felt that they must have a central government with powers granted by formal consent; so, Articles of Confederation were framed by a committee of Congress and presented in due form to the sovereign states. All of them had ratified the Articles by 1781. Thenceforth the thirteen Revolutionary commonwealths possessed a legal agency for united action, the Congress of the Confederation.

In the dark and uncertain days following the

peace of 1783, the American states came to the realization that the Articles of Confederation were not adequate to the needs of the people.   America needed not a confederation of states but a national government.   The Congress of the Confederation was able to provide successfully for organization and management of the national domain beyond the mountains, but it was unable to keep the United States from bankruptcy, to settle the arrears of soldiers' pay, to secure adequate funds for the central government, to open foreign markets to American commerce, to prevent serious conflicts over boundaries and tariffs between the states or disorders within states.   These quarrels convinced Washington and other leading men that only radical changes and improvements in the central government could keep the American states from drifting into helplessness and mutual hostility, easy prey for any aggressive power. The new nation born of the glorious trials and sufferings of the Revolution might be forever lost.

A conference at Mt. Vernon over the commercial rivalry between Virginia and Maryland was the first step in a movement which ended with the Constitutional Convention at Philadelphia, from which there was sent to the states for ratification

a new Constitution of the United States. Strong opposition to the new plan appeared. But resistance from local and particularist interests fell before the weight of Washington's name, the incisive logic of Hamilton's pen, and the widespread argument of influential men that what might not be best for special interests of the states would certainly be good for the American people as a whole. The Constitution was ratified. Elections were held promptly and Washington summoned by unanimous voice to be the first President of the United States. Rhode Island and North Carolina alone remained outside when the new government was organized. They soon perceived, however, the dangers of isolation and joined the Union.

Washington's administration was faced with the labor of establishing principles, precedents, and administrative institutions for the new government. To one task, Alexander Hamilton, Washington's Secretary of the Treasury, set himself zealously and by far reaching financial plans laid the foundations of national credit.

The Articles of Confederation   Volume 13, Chapter III
  Provisions   "   " Pages 174–189
  The slowness of ratification   "   " Pages 57–59

The Critical Period
  Government under the Articles   "   " Chapter IV

The Critical Period—Continued
    The management of the national domain
      The Northwest Ordinance
    The bankruptcy of the United States   Volume 13, Chapter V
      The arrears of soldiers' pay
      Inadequate funds
      The failure of requisitions upon the states
    Conflicting state regulations
  Quarrels and uprisings
    The Wyoming valley
    Vermont   Volume 13, Page 68
    Paper money troubles in Rhode Island   "   Pages 89–90
    Shays' rebellion   "   Pages 93–95

The Movement for a New Constitution
  Conferences over commerce   "   Pages 100–104
    Alexandria
    Annapolis

The Constitutional Convention
  Philadelphia   "   Chapter VI
  Prominent personalities

The Constitution   "   VII
  Rival plans, New Jersey and Virginia
  Features
    The Great Compromise
    The Supreme Law of the Land
    Branches of the National Government
      Executive
      Legislative
      Judicial
    Delegated Powers
      The elastic clause
    Commerce and the Slave Trade
    The Three-fifths Rule
      Slaves

Ratification and Amendment   Volume 13, Chapter VIII
  The procedure in state conventions
    The resistance of Anti-federalists   Volume 43, Pages 1–5
  "The Federalist"
  Adoption by eleven states
  The coercion of Rhode Island and North Carolina
  The first ten amendments   Volume 14, Page 32

The New Government of the United States
  Washington, first President   Volume 14, Chapter I
  Acts of Congress   "   "   II
    The tariff, July 4, 1789
    The creation of departments
      The cabinet
      The judiciary
  Hamilton's financial program   "   "   III
    The building of a strong national government
    The funding of national debts
    The assumption of state debts
      The location of the capital
    Internal revenues
    The national bank
    The mint
    The protection of manufactures

The Doctrine of States Rights
  The theory of strict construction of the Constitution
  Jeffersonian opposition to Hamilton's nationalism
  The Virginia and Kentucky resolutions, 1798
                    Volume 14, Page 219

CHAPTER VII

PROTEST AGAINST EUROPEAN DOMINANCE

THE confederated American states had won their political independence from Great Britain, but foreign powers were by no means ready to accord to them a place as equals in the society of nations. The states were still in economic dependence upon Europe, and European governments did not hesitate to restrict American commerce. It was futile for the Confederation to protest or announce retaliatory measures. Europe did not much care, for it was reasonably certain that the American states would not heed the acts of their own Congress and, even if they did, America was of no great consequence. As Secretary of Foreign Affairs for the Confederation, John Jay sought a settlement with Spain of the problems of trade with Spanish ports, navigation of the Mississippi, and the Florida boundary, but his efforts were in vain. John Adams, as ambassador at London,

was met with the sarcastic but significant query as to the whereabouts of the other twelve representatives of the United States. Thomas Jefferson at Paris enjoyed some of the acclaim that had been Franklin's, but the French government listened to few of his importunities.

The task of the first administration was to secure the respect of the powers for the new nation and to maintain peace while internal affairs were being set in order. The French attempted to use the United States to aid in spreading the French Revolution. They had designs upon the American possessions of decadent Spain. But they were thwarted by Washington's cool reception of Genet. Washington no longer considered binding the obligations of the old alliance of 1778 and declared America's neutrality. Spanish intrigues in the Southwest were thwarted and Western thoughts of separation from the Union were stopped short by the negotiations of Pinckney with the Spanish government. The treaty determined the Florida boundary and opened the Mississippi for ocean-bound commerce. Assured of foreign markets for their surplus grain and other products, the men of Kentucky and Tennessee no longer could charge the East with sacrificing their interests.

In the meantime Washington and Hamilton had attacked the problems left from the peace treaty with Great Britain and despatched John Jay to London. He returned with a treaty which provided for settlement of the problems of debts, Loyalists, northwestern posts, and slaves freed by the British armies, but which was ominously silent on the new questions of impressment and the right to search neutral vessels in time of war. Great Britain was willing to permit American shipping to enter the East Indies and compete for the Oriental trade, but was, as yet, unwilling to give Americans those privileges in the British West Indies that they had once enjoyed as colonial subjects of the Crown. At best Jay's treaty was only a truce; but since it assured the continuance of peace with Great Britain the Senate ratified it with a single reservation in spite of widespread popular disapproval.

France was incensed at the American rapprochement with Great Britain and at Washington's recall of Monroe who was a prominent member of the pro-French party in the United States. When the Federalist Pinckney was sent in his place, France refused to receive the new representative. President Adams attempted to save

the situation by a commission of which Pinckney was a member, but the French dallied and asked a "douceur." The details of the humiliating episode, known as the X. Y. Z. affair, were communicated to Adams and were published by him. The result was the informal war with France of 1798–1800. American frigates met and defeated Frenchmen on the high seas; American privateers took their toll of French commerce; and active preparations were begun to put an army in the field. Over the organization of this army a quarrel developed which opened a dangerous rift in the ranks of the Federalist party. It was closed for the time when President Adams, in answer to a French hint, sent another commission to Paris to meet the representatives of Napoleon just risen to power. In the convention that grew out of the negotiation each party announced fair treatment for the shipping and sailors of the other. With the end of the war came also the end of the Franco-American alliance. From that time till now the United States has never been the ally of any European power.

By 1800 American merchantmen were sailing everywhere busy in every trade. They crowded the ports of Europe, competed with the British for the China trade, and sought profit and adventure

along the coasts of South America and amid the tropical islands of the South Seas. Year after year saw the prosperity of the American shipmasters mount higher and higher. Again war broke out between England and France, and again America remained neutral. For a time the profits of the neutral carrying trade surpassed those of peace. But the prosperity was not for long. Before 1807, the strokes and counter-strokes of the European struggle threatened the Americans with ruin.

*The Diplomatic Weakness of the
        Confederation*   Volume 13, Chapter II
    Economic dependence upon Europe
        Commercial treaties
        Restrictions on American commerce
        Futile efforts to retaliate   "   "   Pages 98–99

Foreign Relations Under the New Government
                                    Volume 14, Chapter V
    The disgrace of tribute
        Barbary commerce-raiders
        Ransom for captive Americans
    The French Revolution and the Franco-
        American alliance   "   "   VI
    The mission of Genet
        War between France and England
        Designs on the Southwest
            The vision of a new French empire
    A warm reception by the American people
    The coolness of the American government
        A choice between treaty obligations and national
            welfare
        The contest between Jefferson and Hamilton

Foreign Relations Under the New Government—Continued
    Washington's proclamation
      The failure of Genet's plans
  The treaty with Spain
    The intrigues of Wilkinson   Volume 18, Pages 260–265
      Indian troubles in the Southwest Volume 14, Pages 86–87
    The attitude of the Westerners
    Pinckney's treaty, 1795   "   Pages 145–146
      The boundary of Florida
      Free navigation of the Mississippi
      The right of deposit at New Orleans
  Negotiations with England   Volume 14, Chapter VII
    The ascendancy of Hamilton
      The mission of Jay
    American complaints and British countercharges
      Violations of the Treaty of 1783 by both parties
      British commercial restrictions
        The West India trade
      The rights of neutrals in the war with France
        The seizure of American vessels
        Impressment
      Indian troubles in the Northwest Volume 14, Pages 93–103
                            Volume 19, Pages 83–96
  Congressional mischief-making   Volume 14, Chapter VII
    The non-intercourse bill in the House
      Defeat in the Senate
  Jay's unsatisfactory treaty
    The cost of peace with Great Britain
    Popular fury
    Acceptance by Congress   Volume 14, Pages 190–192
      The eloquence of Fisher Ames
  American ministers at Paris
    The Federalist, Gouverneur Morris   Pages 117–118
    The Republican, James Monroe   Chapter IX
    The Federalist, C. C. Pinckney
      Rebuff by Revolutionary France
      Seizures of American vessels
    The mission of Pinckney, Marshall, and Gerry
      The humiliating X. Y. Z. Affair

Foreign Relations Under the New Government—Continued
>   Informal war with France
>   "No; no; not a sixpence."
>   The anger of America
>   Naval battles
>   American privateers and French commerce
>   The preparation of an army
>   Wrangles over the command
>   Washington and Hamilton
>   The vexation of Adams
>   New envoys to France
>   The co-operation of Hamilton with Adams
>   Negotiations with Napoleon
>   The Convention of 1800
>   The abrogation of the Franco-American
>   alliance

American competition with European Shipmasters
                                        Volume 36, Chapter IV
>   Trade with the Orient
>   The leadership of Salem
>   Adventures in the tropics   "   "   V
>   "Free Trade and Sailors' Rights"   "   "   VI
>   Neutral trade made the victim of the war between
>   Great Britain and France

CHAPTER VIII

POLITICS AND PARTISANS

ALTHOUGH President Washington was deeply engrossed in grave foreign problems, he was even more concerned over domestic affairs. He hoped to preside over a non-partisan government, but he was soon disillusioned. He gave an aristocratic tone to the etiquette and customs of his high office and in so doing stirred up a swarm of critics who declared that he was false to the democratic spirit of America. When his Secretary of the Treasury, Hamilton, elaborated a financial program which unmistakably was based upon the theory that the new government had powers strongly centralized and national in scope, Washington's administration at once met stubborn resistance from those whose state pride or particular interests would have to be subordinated.

In the factional opposition to Hamilton of Jefferson and his clique the party of opposition, soon

known as the Democratic Republican, had its
origin. After Washington preferred Hamilton's
proposals in regard to Genet's mission, Jefferson
withdrew from the Cabinet to become openly the
leader of the opposition and a candidate for the
presidency in 1796 when Washington would retire.
In the meantime a popular uprising against Hamilton's excise had broken out. Mountaineer farmers
in western Pennsylvania felt that this national
law discriminated against their chief source of
money income, the manufacture of whiskey.
Hamilton's show of military strength easily dis-
persed the rebels. He maintained the supremacy
of the national authority, but he also made many
votes for Jefferson and the Republican party.

The Federalists were strong enough to elect
John Adams as Washington's successor. Jefferson
won second place and the vice-presidency. The
Federalist party, however, was soon torn by a
jealous feud between Adams and Hamilton. The
controversy over the command of the army during
the war with France only widened the breach
between the two factions. They sought, nevertheless, to retain Federalist control of the government by striking down their Republican critics and
assailants with a stringent sedition law. Instead

of silencing their enemies, their persecution of Republican journalists gave to their opponents a legitimate grievance of the greatest political value. To protest against the sedition law, Jefferson and Madison framed the famous Kentucky and Virginia Resolutions. In 1800 their followers rallied to Jefferson at the polls and elevated the Virginian planter to the presidency.

The turn of the political wheel which raised Jefferson to the height of power threw off the Federalist party in broken fragments. It never again gathered itself together in national strength although it was sustained for a quarter-century in New England by sectional interests. Yet in 1800 Jefferson realized that he had won but a partial victory. His party had captured the executive and the legislative branches of the central government, but his opponents still controlled the judiciary where Federalist judges headed by Chief Justice John Marshall enjoyed appointments for life.

Jefferson, therefore, set himself promptly to deprive his opponents of their remaining power. His cabinet contained two men from New England. His program of economical administration would appeal to all property-holders who paid

taxes. His inaugural address held out the olive branch to all individual Federalists. Then, he turned upon those obnoxious leaders of Federalism, the judges. Congress repealed the act which had given so many of them their places. The House of Representatives impeached Justice Chase of the Supreme Court whose remarks in trials under the Sedition Act had exasperated the Republicans. Marshall countered these blows at the judiciary with his famous declaration in *Marbury versus Madison* that the Constitution gave power to the Supreme Court to review legislation of Congress and declare it null and void if it were unconstitutional.

From the beginning the Vice-President had been a sinister figure in the Jeffersonian administration. He had intrigued with a group of reactionary Federalists in New England who were muttering words of disunion, and he had killed in a duel the leading Federalist, Hamilton, who had helped to thwart the scheme. Then, with his political future ruined, he had set out upon a mysterious expedition into the Southwest. Burr's exact motive in this undertaking will probably never be known, but the venture ended in the court house at Richmond, Virginia, with the former Vice-

President on trial for treason. There, to the complete annoyance of Jefferson, Burr was acquitted for want of evidence by the Federalist, Chief Justice Marshall.

Hamiltonian Federalism
 The formation of aristocratic precedents Volume 14, Chapter I
  Official etiquette
  Social customs
 The determination of fundamental
   institutions " " II
  Tariffs — the beginning of protection
  Amendments to the Constitution
  The organization of the Treasury
  The establishment of the Judiciary
 Hamilton's primary policies " " III
  The funding bill
   The national debt
  The assumption of state debts
   Location of the capital
  A national bank
  Excise taxes
  The national mint
  The report on manufactures
 Trials of the President Volume 14, Chapter IV
  Indian troubles and national defence
  Senatorial obstinacy
  State pride
   Hancock, governor of Massachusetts
 Washington's views on education Volume 33, Chapter VII
  A national duty
  His first address to Congress
   A national university
  The national military academy

Jeffersonian Democracy
 Origin in factional opposition to
   Hamilton Volume 14, Chapter VIII

Jeffersonian Democracy—Continued
  Appeals to popular discontent   Volume 43, Pages 5–8
  Jefferson's philosophy   Volume 15, Pages 19–22

The Whiskey Insurrection, 1794 Volume 14, Pages 182–187
 Western mountaineers and the excise
 Hamilton's military demonstration
 The maintenance of national authority

Politics   Volume 14, Pages 187–194
 The disruption of Washington's cabinet
  The resignations of Jefferson and Hamilton
  The intrigue of Randolph
   French influences
 The end of non-partisan government
  Attacks on Washington
  The Farewell Address
 The presidency of John Adams Volume 14, Chapter IX
  The feud with Hamilton
  A Hamiltonian cabinet
  Friendship with Jefferson
 The Alien and Sedition Acts   " Pages 215–221
  War measures
  Opposition by Jeffersonians
   The Kentucky and Virginia Resolutions
    The States Rights theory

The Revolution of 1800   Volume 14, Pages 223–226
 Adams' grudge against Hamiltonians
 The opposition of Hamilton to Adams
 The success of the Jeffersonians
 The decline of Federalism

Jefferson's Reforms
 A Democratic etiquette   Volume 15, Chapter I
 Olive branches for Federalists
  Offices for Democrats
   Appointments from New England
 The triumvirate   " "   II
  Jefferson, Madison, Gallatin
  The formulation of Republican policy

64 THE YALE COURSE OF HOME STUDY

Jefferson's Reforms—Continued
>   Appointments
>   Curtailment of taxes
>   Reduction of the army and navy

Intrigues of Burr and New England Federalists
> Volume 15, Chapter VI
> Plans for a northern confederacy
> The duel between Hamilton and Burr
>   The death of Hamilton
> The ruin of Burr
>   His conspiracy
>   The expedition to the Southwest
>   His associates
>   The traitor, Wilkinson
>   The dupe, Blennerhassett
>   The action of Jefferson
>   Wilkinson in New Orleans
>   The trial of Burr   Volume 16, Chapter IV

The National Judiciary   "   "   I
> John Marshall, Chief Justice   "   "   II
> The attack by Jefferson   "   "   III
>   The repeal of the Federalist Judiciary Act
>   The refusal of Marbury's commission
>   The impeachment of Chase
>   Burr, President of the Senate
>   Jeffersonian bribes
>   The failure to convict Chase
> The resistance of Marshall
>   Great decisions
>   Judicial review
>   Marbury versus Madison, 1803   "   " Pages 66–71
>   Treason
>   The trial of Burr, 1807   "   " Chapter IV

Jeffersonian Ideas of Education   Volume 33, Chapter VI
> State support of free schools
> A free and secular university
>   The University of Virginia
> The Jeffersonian curriculum

CHAPTER IX

THE ESTABLISHMENT OF A NEW NATIONALISM

WHEN John Adams of New England turned over the government to the Virginian planter, Thomas Jefferson, one half of the great task of creating a nation had been well advanced toward completion. The machinery of a central government had been provided in the Constitution and had been set in motion by Washington and Hamilton. By 1801, it was functioning with considerable efficiency. If the new United States, however, were to look forward to stability and permanent independence, something more than merely an efficient government would be needed. Political independence must be supplemented by economic self-sufficiency. This did not mean that all trade ties with the outer world should be broken; on the contrary, they must be strengthened. It did mean, however, that the people of America should, in an emergency, be able to produce all the food, raw materials, and

65

manufactured articles necessary to maintain the life of the nation unimpaired. It fell to the lot of the Democratic-Republicans, led by Jefferson and Madison, to guide the American people through such an emergency.

A foretaste of the difficulties ahead was given by the increased insolence and aggressiveness of the Barbary pirates who seemed able to jeopardize American commerce at will. The time came, almost at the outset of Jefferson's administration, when the United States could no longer brook this menace. After a display of American naval power, the corsairs were willing to make fair promises. While Decatur and Bainbridge were active in the Mediterranean the settlers of Kentucky and Tennessee were watching with growing apprehension the return of the vast territory of Louisiana from Spanish to French control. Napoleon had secured possession of the mouth of the Mississippi. President Jefferson promptly undertook to purchase the island of New Orleans from the Corsican, in order that Americans might deposit their goods while they were being transferred from river boats to ocean-going ships. But Louisiana had suddenly become less attractive to the French, and Napoleon sold the whole territory to the amazed Americans.

So the stage was set for that population movement across the broad valley of the Mississippi which was one of the most striking episodes in the history of the United States. The Americans had scarcely grasped their good fortune when they found themselves caught in the maelstrom of a world war.

England and France were again at war, and this time there was to be no respite until Napoleon had fallen. At first the war brought prosperity to the American shipmasters who became the leading neutral traders. But there were insults and injuries on the high seas from both belligerents. By 1807 these had become unbearable. The peaceful Jefferson retaliated. By an economic boycott, he hoped to starve Europe into a respect for American rights. But his efforts failed to keep the United States out of war. For five years the troubles continued; then the young "war hawks" who had come out of the West forced the weak President Madison into decisive action. The West coveted Florida and Canada and was bitter against the British for their incitement of Indian raids on frontier settlements. The United States declared war.

With an empty treasury and military affairs in a muddle, the United States set out to conquer

Canada and combat the British fleet on the high seas. Disaster awaited the American armies in Canada. The British navy ultimately bottled up American merchantmen and warships in port but not until the union jack had been hauled down from more than one proud frigate and American privateers had become the scourge of the British merchant fleet. In the treaty of peace were mentioned none of the important issues which had brought on the war. Yet events proved that it marked the end of an era.

The second war with England, itself, profoundly affected American life. The United States had been practically cut off from the manufactures of Europe. On the Atlantic slope, particularly in maritime New England, industries to supply the resulting need had sprung up. Eastern manufacturers took a new and lively interest in the West where lay a constantly expanding market for their wares. In addition, the end of war in Europe cleared the seas of hostile warships and allowed the American merchant marine to develop unmolested. To the people who lived on the plains west of the mountains, the War of 1812 gave opportunity to destroy the military power of strong Indian tribes east of the Mississippi and thus to

open for settlement large areas of fertile land. The war removed the British threat on the northern frontier and on the south gave opportunity to force the Spaniard out of West Florida. This paved the way for the ultimate purchase of East Florida. America, which had hitherto looked toward Europe, now turned squarely about to face the West and, ignoring to a large extent the affairs of the world, bent to the task of creating a nation in a wilderness.

It was the beginning of a new national consciousness, a feeling of self-sufficiency and isolation. Throwing aside for the moment the sectionalism which had led New England to the verge of secession at the Hartford Convention, the American people sought to bind the agricultural sections of the West with the industrial section in the East and stand apart from the world. The old Federalist party which had retired from the national position of Hamilton upon the sectional interest of New England was broken and discredited.

The new nationalism was voiced in the decisions of Chief Justice Marshall which again and again asserted the supremacy of the federal over state governments. President Monroe proclaimed it to

the world in the doctrine which Americans have
come to call the cornerstone of their foreign policy.
In the field of literature and learning, as well, this
new nationalism was given expression. American
men of letters at last received a European audience.
American educators began to construct the school
system which has become so typical of American
nationhood.

American Commerce and Barbary Pirates

Volume 15, Chapter III

Captain Bainbridge and tribute
The blockade of Tripoli
  The Philadelphia
    Bainbridge, captive
    The exploit of Decatur
  The bombardment of the Pasha's stronghold
The adventure of William Eaton
  An international army
    The march across the desert
    The capture of Derne
Lear's treaty
  The purchase of peace

The Acquisition of Louisiana "   "   IV
The Treaty of San Ildefonso, 1800
  Retrocession to France
  Alarm in America
    The restoration of a French empire
The importance of San Domingo
  Toussaint L'Ouverture
    Revolt from France
The advances of Jefferson
  An offer for the island of New Orleans
    The interests of the western settlers

The Acquisition of Louisiana—Continued
    The withdrawal of the right of deposit by the
        Spanish authorities
   The special mission of Monroe
  Napoleon's change of plans
   The offer to Livingston
   The purchase by the United States
    Boundaries
    Government
    The constitutionality of the purchase
                     Volume 43, Page 8

Neutral Rights in the Napoleonic Wars
  British practices   Volume 15, Chapter VII
    Desertion from the Royal Navy
    Refuge on American merchantmen
  Impressment   Volume 36, Pages 107–116
    The right of search
    The right of expatriation
  Restrictions on the West India trade
    The Rule of 1756
     "Broken voyages"
    The case of the Essex, 1805
  The Leander incident, 1806
    The wrath of the American people
    Jefferson's proclamation
  The affair of the Chesapeake and Leopard, 1807
    National fury
    Jefferson indignant but not martial

Jeffersonian Pacificism and Peaceable Coercion
                     Volume 15, Chapter VIII
  Monroe, ambassador to Great Britain
  Commercial restrictions, the American weapon
  William Pinkney, co-laborer with Monroe
    Negotiations
      Restoration of trade with the French West Indies
      Abolition of impressment
      Indemnity for seizures under the Essex ruling
    Jefferson's disgust with their first agreement

Jeffersonian Pacificism and Peaceable Coercion—Continued
    The second negotiation
      Reparation for the Chesapeake
      Abolition of impressment
        The sarcasm of Canning
  The struggle between Great Britain and France
   Effects on neutral trade
    The British blockade of French ports
     Successive Orders-in-Council
   French retaliation
    Napoleonic decrees
      Berlin, 1806
      Milan, 1807
   The American defence against Great Britain
    The embargo, 1807
      Napoleonic irony
        The Bayonne decree, 1808
     The effect of the embargo
       Evasion and violation by American citizens
  The failure of peaceable coercion
   The repeal of the embargo
    The Non-Intercourse Act, 1809
  Madison, successor of Jefferson   Volume 15, Chapter IX
   British ministers at Washington
    Erskine's promises
     Repudiation by Great Britain
     Jackson's failure
  A Congressional way of escape
   Macon's Bill No. 2
    Napoleon's response
     Revocation of his decrees
     Continued confiscation
  Madison's ill-advised decision
   His acceptance of Napoleonic promises
   Restrictions directed against Great Britain
    Painful misgivings
     The ebb of confidence in Madison
  The reconstruction of the cabinet
   The elimination of the Smith faction

Jeffersonian Pacificism and Peaceable Coercion—Continued
       The retention of Gallatin
     The alliance with the chief opposition
      Monroe, Secretary of State
        Tacit promise of the presidency
       A stronger front toward Europe
    The rise of the war spirit in America
     The affair of the President and the Little Belt
      Vengeance for the Chesapeake
     The discomfiture of the new British minister
      The disavowal of the Leopard

The War Hawks
  Western aggressiveness
   Desire for Florida
  Bitterness toward Great Britain
   Contempt for British strength in Canada
  "Free Trade and Sailors' Rights" in the background
  British collusion with the Indians
   The menace to the frontier
    The battle of Tippecanoe, 1811
      Harrison and Tecumseh   Volume 19, Chapter VIII
  Pressure upon Madison
   The renomination
   The declaration of war with Great Britain
    British repeal of the Orders-in-Council

The War of 1812
  Distress at Washington   Volume 15, Chapter XI
   Inadequate preparation
   Incompetence of the executive
   Bankruptcy of the Treasury
   Disaffection of New England
    The Hartford Convention, 1814 Volume 19, Pages 151–160
  Military aspects of the war   Volume 17, Chapter I
   The invasions of Canada
    Hull against Brock at Detroit, 1812
     British control of the Northwest
    Harrison against Procter in Upper
     Canada, 1813   Volume 17, Chapter II

The War of 1812—Continued
    The assistance of Perry on Lake Erie
    The battle of the Thames
      The death of Tecumseh

  Campaigns about Niagara and Lake
      Ontario   Volume 17, Chapter IV
    Defeat at Queenston Heights, 1812
    The failure of Dearborn on Lake Ontario,
      May, 1813
    Brown's defence of Sackett's Harbor, 1813
  Operations against Montreal, Nov., 1813
    Wilkinson down the St. Lawrence
    Hampton from Lake Champlain
    The fiasco of Chrystler's Farm
The year 1814
  The last invasion of Canada
    Brown and Scott across Niagara River
      Chippewa
      Lundy's Lane
  The British advance on Lake Champlain
    The blunders of Armstrong
    Prevost before Plattsburg
      Macdonough's defence
      The retirement of the British
  British operations in Chesapeake Bay   "   " X
    Bladensburg
    The burning of Washington
    The bombardment of Baltimore
      The Star Spangled Banner
  American campaigns in the Southwest
                    Volume 20, Chapter II
    Desire for West Florida   Volume 17, Chapter X
    Tecumseh's visit to the Creeks
    The massacre of Fort Mims
    Horseshoe Bend, 1814
    Jackson in Florida
    The British at Pensacola
    The battle of Mobile

The War of 1812—Continued
   Jackson's frontiersmen
    The battle of New Orleans, Jan. 8, 1815
 Naval aspects of the war
  Perry's victory on Lake Erie, 1813 Volume 17, Chapter III
   Strategic importance
    The safety of the Northwest
  American frigates on the high seas "   " V
   The Constitution
    The escape from the British fleet
    The duel with the Guerrière
   The United States   " I " VI
    The fight with the Macedonian
    The Constitution and the Java
   The Chesapeake   "   " VII
    The defeat by the Shannon
   The Essex   "   " VIII
  British naval policy   Pages 140–150
   Convoys for merchant fleets
   Fleet maneuvers
    The blockade of American ports
    The capture of the President
  American privateers   Volume 36, Chapter VII
    The "Blockade of London"
   Roamers in the English Channel and the Irish Sea
    The destruction of British commerce
  Macdonough's victory on Lake Champlain
   Strategic importance   Volume 17, Chapter IX
    Safety for New England and
     New York   Pages 175–184

The Treaty of Peace   Volume 15, Chapter XII
 The negotiators at Ghent
  Clashing personalities
 British demands for an Indian state between Canada
  and the United States
 The questions of boundaries, impressment, fisheries,
  navigation of the Mississippi, slave trade
 Effect of the news from Bladensburg and Plattsburg

The Treaty of Peace—Continued
    The opinion of the Duke of Wellington
  Terms of the settlement
    "Peace — and nothing more?"   Volume 36, Pages 131–132

Succeeding conventions:

Following the peace of Ghent, Great Britain and the United States came to three agreements. The commercial convention of 1815 provided for reciprocal trade between the United States and the British Isles and between the United States and British East Indian possessions. Great Britain still denied to the American people the trade that, as subjects of the Crown, they had once enjoyed with the British West Indies. The agreement of 1817 provided for disarmament of the Great Lakes. The convention of 1818 made regulations for American participation in the shore fisheries of Labrador, it ran the Canadian boundary from the Lake of the Woods along the 49° latitude to the Rocky Mountains, and stipulated that the Oregon country beyond should be held in joint occupation for ten years.

The New Nationalism   Volume 20, Pages 138–139
  Monroe, Nationalist President   Volume 43, Pages 8–10
    His election   Volume 15, Chapter XIII
    His cabinet
      Adams, Secretary of State
      Calhoun, Secretary of War
        The disappointment of Clay
    The bargain for Florida
      Jackson in Florida   Volume 20, Chapter III
      The Spaniard, Callava
      The triumph of Adams
  The growth of a nation   Volume 19, Pages 160–171
    The birth of new states
    The development of transportation
      The steamboat   Volume 21, Chapter VII
      The Cumberland Road   "   " VIII
        Internal Improvements
          Madison's veto
            Calhoun's Bonus Bill   Volume 20, Page 139
  The Erie Canal

The New Nationalism—Continued
  Chief Justice Marshall's doctrine of nationalism
    The national bank   Volume 16, Chapter V
      McCulloch versus Maryland, 1819
    Interstate commerce
      Gibbons versus Ogden, 1824
    Foreign commerce
      Brown versus Maryland, 1826
    The rights of property
      Fletcher versus Peck, 1810   "   "   VI
      The Dartmouth College Case, 1819
    The restriction of state sovereignty   "   "   VII
      Martin versus Hunter's Lessee, 1816
        Decision by Story
      Cohens versus Virginia, 1821
      Craig versus Missouri, 1830
      Georgia and the Indian cases, 1830–1832
    Marshall in private life   "   "   VIII
  The foreign policy of the new nation   Volume 15, Chapter XIV
    Zeal for emancipation of South America
      from Spanish control
    Impatience with British claims in Oregon
    Counters to Russian claims on the Pacific
    The problem of Cuba
    The plans of the Holy Alliance
      Rejection by Great Britain
      British overtures to the United States
    A separate course—The Monroe Doctrine
                    Volume 46, Chapter I
      The European system
        No further colonization in America
        No interference with American republics
      The American system
        No meddling with European affairs
        No interference with existing colonies in America
      Conclusions
        Two separate worlds
        The United States, leader in the western world
          The self-appointed guardian

A European Audience for American Men of Letters
Volume 34, Chapter V

America become articulate
  The North American Review
Washington Irving
  His vogue in England
  His sojourn in Spain
James Fenimore Cooper
  A contemporary rival of Scott
William Cullen Bryant
  Poet and journalist

The Schools of the New Nation   Volume 33, Chapter VIII
  The public school system
    School districts
  Secondary schools
    Academies and high schools
  Textbooks
    Noah Webster's speller
    Jedediah Morse's geography
  Great educators
    Horace Mann's contribution   "   "   IX
      The Massachusetts Board
        Mann's reports
      The training of teachers
        Normal schools
      The President of Antioch College
    Henry Barnard
      His services to Connecticut
      The Chancellor of Wisconsin University
  DeWitt Clinton and the free school   "   "   X
    The Free School Society
      Opposition to sectarian schools
    The contest in Pennsylvania
      Thaddeus Stevens

CHAPTER X

SECTIONALISM AND JACKSONIAN DEMOCRACY

ALTHOUGH the task of creating an efficient central government had been practically completed and the foundations of economic self-sufficiency firmly laid, the people of America still faced difficult work. Theirs was a country of great distances; it took weeks, sometimes months, to travel on horseback and by stage-coach from outlying communities to the national capital. The broad barrier of the Appalachians divided the country into East and West; climatic differences created a North and South. The frontiersmen were ever on the move westward. Even before the presidency of Jackson, pioneers had settled beyond the Mississippi and advanced toward the towering Rockies. As the new nation finally shook off its dependence upon Europe, it faced the problem of preventing disintegration at home. Each section possessed an area sufficient for the creation of a nation of

respectable size, measured by European standards, and had peculiar interests that made such a development far from unlikely.

As the restless elements of New England and the Old South moved westward the contrast of sectional interests came into sharp relief. New Englanders soon outnumbered the earlier pioneers from the South in the new states north of the Ohio and east of the Mississippi. The Northwest became a land of small farms and little manufacturing industries based upon free labor. The cotton planters of the Old South advanced into the Gulf region and modified the earlier frontier society. Alabama and Mississippi became cotton-producing states dependent upon the plantation system and slave labor. The competition of New Englanders and Southerners for the West came to a deadlock over the admission of Missouri as a slave state. The resulting compromise maintained the balance of northern and southern representation in the Senate of the United States, but did not banish the specter of disintegration.

The flame of nationalism still mounted high. The Federalist party, discredited by its sectional opposition to the War of 1812, had ceased to be of national significance in 1814. During the two

administrations of Monroe, America had one political party, the Democratic-Republican party of
Jefferson. It was the "era of good feeling."
Under the surface, however, the Jeffersonian organization was breaking into factions centered
about rival leaders, each leader representing a
section. Out of the turmoil were eventually to
rise two new parties, Democratic and Whig. The
storm broke in 1824 when five aspirants sought the
presidency. John Quincy Adams stood as the
candidate of New England, Calhoun of the Old
South, Clay for the West, and Crawford as heir to
the Virginian succession. The fifth claimant to
recognition was Andrew Jackson. The victorious
commander at New Orleans paraded before the
country as a national hero. In reality, he typified
the rugged democracy, the social and economic
equality of the frontier, for as yet the West was
not definitely broken into Northern and Southern
areas. Jacksonian Democracy was a manifesta-
tion of nationalism only in the sense that the
interests of the West must be seen as the best
interests of the nation. Jackson secured the
largest popular vote, but he was deprived of the
presidency. Adams and Clay joined to place the
New Englander in the White House. Clay

became Secretary of State. Jackson's followers swore revenge for the "corrupt bargain" and began immediately to construct a party-machine that would control the next election.

Although he had won the presidency by a sectional coalition, Adams strove to make his administration national in character; but he, in turn, was overthrown by an alliance of sections. Calhoun became Jackson's running mate for the campaign of 1828. The cotton planters of the Old South joined with the frontiersmen from beyond the mountains to form the new Democratic party. For eight years Jackson maintained political mastery such as few presidents have achieved while his party enjoyed the spoils of partisan government. The Old South had expected that Jackson would break down the tariff walls built by the protectionist interests of Clay and Adams. Jackson's nationalism, however, was not hollow sound. When some of his allies in the Old South threatened to nullify the national tariff law, he joined with his political opponents, Clay and Webster, to put down this menace to the nation. But he opposed them, at the same time, in his war upon the Bank of the United States. This institution, enjoying a monopoly of national finance

and paying its dividends to Eastern aristocrats and foreign capitalists, made an admirable victim for the altar of western democracy.

Jackson, abandoning Calhoun and the southern planters, designated Martin Van Buren as his successor and secured his election in 1836. It fell to his lot to reap the whirlwind that the Jacksonian policies had sown in destroying the Bank and encouraging the "pet banks" to speculate with national funds. The Panic of 1837, in part the result of such unsound measures, paralyzed the country's business. As a remedy for national distress, Van Buren urged the establishment of the Sub-treasury system to safeguard public funds. With some modification that system has remained to the present time. Jackson also left to Van Buren the necessity of grasping the Texan nettle. If he did not recognize revolutionary Texas as independent of Mexico, the slave holders of the South and the expansionists of the West would turn upon him. If he did so, the wrath of the East where antislavery opinions were growing would be aroused. Van Buren chose the latter course as the lesser danger. Jackson handed on to his successor a third problem, the continuance of Jacksonian Democracy in power. In 1836, the

opponents of Jacksonism had found a common name as Whigs, but the rival factions had been unable to decide upon a single candidate. By 1840, however, they united in the choice of General William Henry Harrison, a military hero, representing the nationalist enthusiasm of the West. With an uproarious campaign for "True Democracy," in which hard cider flowed abundantly, the Whigs drove Van Buren and the Jacksonians from power.

The Sharpening of Sectional Consciousness
  The specter of slavery   Volume 28, Chapter I
    The colonial inheritance
    The doctrine of the American Revolution
    The compromise of the Constitution
    Geographical division
      Changing sentiments
        The economic basis of slavery
          Cotton
        The prohibition of the slave trade
  The Missouri Compromise   Volume 15, Chapter XV
    A "reprieve"
  Clashing interests   Volume 19, Chapter X
    North and South   Volume 15, Pages 311–313
      The split of the Southwest from the Northwest
        Cotton culture versus small farming and
          manufacturing
    The newer Northwest
      The dominance of migration from New England
    Issues
      Internal improvements
      Tariffs
      The national bank

The Sharpening of Sectional Consciousness—Continued
   Local forms of government
   Slavery
     Schemes of compromise from the Northwest

The Figure of Andrew Jackson
 The frontiersman   Volume 20, Chapter I
 The general
  Against the British   "   " II
  Against the Spanish   "   " III
   The Rhea letter
   Official censure
     Private satisfaction   Volume 15, Pages 278–280
     Jackson's campaign at Washington
      The antagonism of Clay
 The governor of Florida   Volume 20, Chapter III

The Election of 1824   "   " IV
 Personal politics in the "Era of Good Feeling"
  The national hero, Jackson Compare Volume 43, Pages 8–10
   His political managers
  The rivalry of the sections
   Adams for New England
   Crawford, heir to the Virginian succession
   Calhoun, representative of the Old South
   Clay, "Harry of the West"
  The passing of the Congressional caucus
          Compare Volume 43, Pages 22–23
  Nominations by state legislatures
  Canvass by political managers
   The creation of the Jacksonian machine
   Calhoun's alliance with Jackson
    The nomination of the Pennsylvania convention
     The "Keystone state"
   Jackson's procession toward Washington
   News of the returns
 The deadlock
  Election by the House of Representatives
   The alliance of Clay with Adams

The Election of 1824—Continued
>> The charge of "corrupt bargain"
>> The selection of Adams over Jackson

The Coalition of Adams and Clay in Power Volume 20, Chapter V
> Popular disapproval   Pages 95–106
>> The growing demand for election of presidents by
>> the people
>> The effect of the "corrupt bargain"
>> The Puritan as President
>> Baffled spoilsmen
>> Adams' conception of the civil service
> Adams' program: liberal construction of the Constitution
>> National expenditures for roads and canals
>> A national university
>> Protective tariffs
>> Sale of public lands at market price
>>> Proceeds for general welfare
>> The Panama Congress
>>> Conference with South American republics
>>>> The reluctance of Adams
>>>> The influence of Clay
> Jacksonian opposition
>> Plans for 1828
>> Jackson, personal leader of his campaign
>>> His following
>>>> Western Democrats
>>>> Calhoun's followers
>>>> Crawford's old supporters
>>>>> Van Buren and the New York contingent
> Adams, Georgia, and the Indians   Volume 20, Pages 201–208
>> The compact of 1802
>>> Georgia and the United States
>> The Indian Springs Treaty of 1825
>> Governor Troup and the President
>> New Treaties with the Creeks

The Tariff of Abominations and the Election of 1828
> Changing opinions in South Carolina Volume 20, Chapter VIII

The Tariff of Abominations and the Election of 1828—Continued
    The effect of competition with new cotton lands
      on the Gulf   Volume 20, Pages 158–163
    The burden of protective tariffs
      The tariff of 1824
      The proposals of 1827
  The scheme of 1828
  Its failure
  The alliance of Calhoun and Jackson
    The hopes of the Old South
    The election of 1828   "   Pages 106–112
                      Volume 43, Pages 11–12

Jacksonian Democracy in Power   Volume 20, Chapter VI
  The court of King Andrew
    Suppliants seeking offices
    The day of the common man
      Jackson's inauguration
    His cabinet
      Van Buren, Secretary of State
      The Kitchen Cabinet
  Jackson's conception of the civil service
    The clean sweep
      Rotation in office
  Calhoun overshadowed by Van Buren
    Talk of Jackson's second term
      Breach of promise to Calhoun
      "The Little Magician"
    The Eaton affair
    The revelation of Calhoun's part in Monroe's censure
      of Jackson, 1818
  Jackson's break with Calhoun, 1830
    Reorganization of the cabinet
  The great debate   Volume 20, Chapter VII
    Webster for the North and Union
    Hayne for the South and States Rights
      The contest of political theories
      The stakes
        The adherence of the West

People now knew what Webster and the East had for reply to Hayne and the Old South. What would be the response of western democracy and its President, Andrew Jackson? Jackson dismayed the Old South with his famous toast: "Our Union!— It must be preserved!"

Nullification and Compromise

The grievance of South Carolina
  Rising tariffs
  The declining price of cotton
Means of resistance: Nullification
  The compact theory and state sovereignty
    Calhoun's Exposition, 1828
The riddle of Jackson's opinion
  His toast to the Union, April 12, 1830
  Calhoun's reply
The struggle of South Carolina
  Division within the state
  The tariff proposals of 1832
  The Convention, Nov. 19, 1832
    The ordinance of nullification
  Jackson's proclamation, Dec. 10
    Calhoun's resignation of the Vice-Presidency
      Senator from South Carolina
  Warlike preparations
    Refusal of other Southern states to join South
      Carolina
  Jackson's Force Bill
The way of escape
  New tariff legislation
    The Verplanck bill
    Clay's Compromise of 1833
      Reduction by stages until 1842
  The end of nullification
    The object of attack gone
    Nullification of the Force Bill
    The victory undecided

Destruction of the National Bank   Volume 20, Chapter IX
  An aristocratic institution

Destruction of the National Bank—Continued
    The record of the Second Bank of the United States
    Democratic venom
      The uncertainty of Jackson's opinion
      The resistance of Biddle
        The Portsmouth affair
        The campaign in Congress, 1832
          The re-charter bill
          Jackson's veto

Antimasonry:

A third party entered the national campaign of 1832. The mysterious disappearance of William Morgan in Western New York during 1826 was blamed upon the Masonic order. The resulting tumult gave opportunity for a few leaders to organize the protest of the community against Masonry into a political party for the purpose of overturning the established order. Antimasonry spread rapidly into Pennsylvania and New England. It gathered up discontented elements from every quarter to champion reform. Its candidate for the presidency in 1832 was William Wirt, once attorney general under Monroe. The Antimasons held a national nominating convention in 1831, and since then, national party conventions have been in general use.

The presidential election of 1832
    The rise of the national nominating convention
            Volume 43, Pages 16, 23–27

    Clay against Jackson
      Issue: the Bank   Volume 40, Page 27
      The triumph of Jackson
    Jackson's mandate from the people
    Removal of the deposits, 1833
      McLane, Duane, and Taney
    The pet banks
    Senatorial censure
    The end of the Bank

Jackson, Georgia, and the Indians   Volume 20, Chapter X
    Inheritance from Adams
      The Cherokee problem

Jackson, Georgia, and the Indians—Continued
      Discovery of gold
        The horde of white men
   Jackson's convictions
     Removal to the West
     His support of Georgia
   Marshall's decisions   Volume 16, Pages 193–197
     Protection for the Indian
     Jackson's refusal to enforce the decision of the Court
   Georgia's nullification

Whereas Jackson was vehement in opposition to nullification of a federal statute by South Carolina, he ignored Georgia's nullification of a federal judicial decision. Perhaps personal antipathies toward Calhoun, leader of nullification in South Carolina, and Marshall, Chief Justice of the United States, explain even if they do not reconcile the inconsistencies of the President.

The Indian migrations across the Mississippi
                      Volume 20, Pages 214–216
   Treaties of cession
   The Indian Territory
     The Black Hawk War, 1832

Jackson and Foreign Affairs

The United States had failed in repeated attempts since the Revolution to gain admission for its vessels into the direct trade with the British West Indies. The administration of John Quincy Adams had neglected to take advantage of an offer from Great Britain, and it had been withdrawn. Jackson's administration reopened negotiations and conducted them so skilfully that at last American vessels were allowed to participate in the West Indian trade.

Jackson also secured a settlement of claims against France arising out of depredations upon American commerce during the Napoleonic wars. Under the reign of Louis Philippe in 1831, France agreed to a treaty, but the French chamber of deputies made no appropriation of funds to meet the payments agreed upon. Jackson controlled his irritation until 1834 and then

recommended to Congress reprisals upon French property. France became angry, recalled its minister, and demanded an apology from Jackson. He remained firm but gave France a loophole for escape from humiliation. Great Britain's offer of mediation was accepted and the American claims soon paid.

Martin Van Buren   Volume 20, Chapter XI
  The retirement of Jackson
  The succession of 1836
    The platform: Jackson's record
    The man: Van Buren
      His career   Volume 43, Pages 27–33
      The opposition
        The beginnings of the Whig party
                  Volume 20, Pages 225–227

        Four sectional candidates
          Webster in New England
          Harrison in the Northwest
          White in the Southwest
          McLean in Ohio
    The election of Van Buren
  His administration   Volume 20, Pages 199–200
    The whirlwind: the panic of 1837
      Jackson's financial policy
      Pet banks
        Land sales
          The specie circular, July 11, 1836
      Van Buren's remedy
        The Independent Treasury
  The Texan nettle   Volume 24, Chapter V
    The recognition of Texan independence
      Jackson's hesitancy
      Van Buren's responsibility
        The opposition of New England to the exten-
        sion of slave territory
      The part of Great Britain
      Investments in Mexico
      Annexation of Texas to the United States least
      desirable

Jacksonian Rule in Jeopardy
  The problem of Van Buren's re-election
                                     Volume 20, Pages 232–233
    The little aristocrat from New York
    Harrison and the Whigs
      A military hero
      "True Democracy"
  The campaign of 1840
    For the Whigs — "Down with Van Burenism"
      "Tippecanoe and Tyler Too"
    For the Democrats
      The record of twelve years
    The Liberty Party   Volume 28, Pages 88–89
      Political abolitionists
      Omen of the future
  The election of Harrison
  "An Indignation President"

The career of the Whigs   Volume 20, Page 200
                                    Volume 28, Chapters VI, VII
                                    Volume 24, Pages 106, 157–159
                                    Volume 27, Pages 125–127

Harrison died a month after his inauguration. Tyler, an old "States Rights" Democrat whose opposition to Jackson had placed him among the Whigs, became President. But Clay considered himself the director of Whig policies and announced the program: repeal of the sub-treasury law, creation of a national bank, and restoration of protective tariffs. Tyler gave his assent to the first measure but opposed the others so firmly that Clay's followers read the President out of the Whig party. Tyler then took Calhoun and pro-slavery Democrats into his administration.

In the campaign of 1844, Clay was the Whig candidate. He attempted to hold the middle ground that the annexation of Texas would not necessarily mean the extension of slavery. Both Northern and Southern men lost confidence in him. With a frank demand for national expansion Polk won the election for the Democratic party. In opposition to Polk's administration the Whigs vainly resisted the re-establishment of the sub-

treasury system and the reduction of tariff duties. When war with Mexico broke out, "conscience Whigs" in the North urged the Wilmot Proviso that territories acquired from Mexico should not be open for the extension of slavery.

The Whig party evaded the slavery issue in the presidential campaign of 1848 and nominated the military hero, General Zachary Taylor. Many northern Whigs bolted from the party to form a coalition with anti-slavery Democrats, the Free Soil party, in support of Van Buren. His candidacy hurt the chances of the regular Democratic nominee, Cass, and assured the election of Taylor. Once more in control of the national government, the Whigs were obliged to settle the controversy over the territory acquired from Mexico. Clay's compromise measures arranged for such a settlement but included a stringent fugitive slave law which "conscience Whigs" could never obey. But Southern Whigs insisted that the Compromise of 1850 must be final. On that rock the Whig party met shipwreck. Party leaders endeavored to steer the party through the treacherous waters. Georgian Whigs wrote the party platform of 1852. The nomination was given to another military hero, General Winfield Scott. But enough Southern Whigs abandoned the party to throw the election to the Democratic "dark horse," General Pierce of New Hampshire. The Whig party never again put a candidate in the field. Young Whigs in the North joined the new Republican party. Older Whigs turned half-heartedly to the Know Nothing party and supported Fillmore in the election of 1856. Then they joined the Constitutional Union party of 1860. In the South, old Whigs had a momentary sojourn in the Know Nothing party, but sooner or later united with the Democrats.

CHAPTER XI

COMMERCE, INDUSTRY, AND THE TARIFF TO THE CIVIL WAR

THE four and one half decades that elapsed between the Peace of Ghent and the outbreak of the Civil War saw great changes in the commercial and industrial life of America. Packet ships from Boston to New York hurried back and forth across the Atlantic on regular schedules. Great clipper ships, the glory of the old merchant marine, rounded Cape Horn, looked in at San Francisco in the days of the gold rush, and vied with all comers for the trade of the Orient. Whalers from Sag Harbor, Nantucket, and New Bedford could be found on every ocean. Few were the sea-lanes that did not know the American flag in the Forties and Fifties. In the same years that Yankee clippers were establishing contact with the ports of the world, home-staying Americans were binding the nation together with improved communication.

With the opening of the Nineteenth Century came the first good roads movement which created, particularly in the East, a network of turnpikes. The great Cumberland road across the mountains bound the seaboard to the rich interior lowland. The canal followed hard upon the heels of the new highway and, in 1825, when a line of cannon from Buffalo to New York boomed out the completion of the Erie Canal, opened a new era in transportation. East and West alike felt the change. State after state became familiar with the canal boat and the tow-path. Already had begun the utilization of the vast river system of the Mississippi Valley. From the days of the first Kentucky settlements, flat boats and keel boats had floated down the Ohio and the Mississippi bearing produce and immigrants. With the coming of the steamboat, new monsters appeared upon the inland rivers carrying heavy cargoes between the Northwest and the South.

In the latter region, following the invention of the cotton gin in 1793, cotton growing had spread from the Atlantic coast plain, first to the uplands of the Piedmont, and then on into the rich country of Alabama, Mississippi, and Louisiana. With cotton had gone the plantation system and slav-

ery. When the Eighteenth Century ended, it seemed as though slavery was doomed, but the prosperity founded on cotton gave it new life. Southern leaders, from apologizing for it as a necessary evil, came to look upon it as a positive good.

While Southern culture was spreading through the Southwest, a transformation was occurring in the North and East. Industrialism had made its appearance shortly before the War of 1812, and the new factory was appearing from New England to the Ohio Valley. Industry brought with it the problem of labor. Streams of immigrants from Europe fed the mills of America with unskilled workmen who congregated in towns and cities in little foreign groups unfamiliar with American ways. It was inevitable that class-consciousness should develop and that the laborers, individually weak, should attempt collective action to gain their ends, shorter hours and more pay. In the hard times of 1837 many of these early unions went to pieces but, as the country recovered and work became more plentiful, labor organizations again became active. Here and there in America during this period of growth appeared utopian experiments, communistic societies of the literati at

Brook Farm and of common folk in New Harmony.

The country was more amused than alarmed over these social experiments, but the problem of the tariff which was so interwoven with the social and political life of the people was no trivial matter. From the beginning under the Constitution, the principle of protection for American industries had entered into public policy. When the wave of nationalist feeling swept over the land after the War of 1812, protection became the cardinal doctrine of Henry Clay's "American System." When the coalition of Clay and Adams came to power, the promotion of the industrial interests of their sections was assured. The controversy over high tariffs grew intense. Protection became one of the chief issues in the election of 1828. The South expected that Jackson would check the protectionist movement. But Jackson did not put a stop to Congressional pyramiding of tariff duties. Some of his allies in the Old South broke away from his party. Calhoun tried, in 1832, the weapon of nullification to defend the interests of his section. Clay then brought forward his compromise plan of a ten-year truce. Protection was to be whittled down gradually. At the end of the

decade, however, Clay sought to restore the protective principle to former vigor. The tariff of 1842 provided for an increase of duties, but the Democratic victory of 1844 put an end to Clay's plans. Thereafter the Democratic tariffs of 1846 and 1857 were the law of the land, and they looked away from protection toward the ideal of free trade. On the eve of the Civil War, the new Republican party made good its maiden promises to the manufacturers. The Morrill tariff, portent of the future, definitely aimed to establish the protective principles.

Ocean Transportation   Volume 36, Chapter VIII
  The packet ships of the forties
    The first liners to Europe
      American ships and officers
      Foreign crews
    Displacement by steamers
      English competition
        Cunard versus Collins
        The failure of Congress to meet British subsidies
  The age of the clipper ship   Volume 36, Chapter IX
    American supremacy
      Successful competition with British merchantmen
        in the Orient
      The tea trade
    The California gold rush
      The voyage around Cape Horn
      The scarcity of deep-water sailors
        The trials of a skipper
          Ruffian crews

Ocean Transportation—Continued
    The effect of the Panic of 1857 and the Civil War
      The demoralization of American shipping
  The whalers of New Bedford   Volume 36, Pages 179–184
  The coastwise trade   "   Chapter X
    Fishing on the Grand Banks
    Yankee shipmasters in Southern ports

Inland Transportation
  The development before the use of steam
    Rivers   Volume 21, Chapter III
    Wagon roads   "   "   IV
    The flatboat trade   "   "   V
      River settlements   "   "   VI
  The coming of steam   "   "   VII
    Fulton and others   Volume 37, Pages 53–69
  The penetration of the Appalachian Range
         Volume 21, Chapter VIII
    The Cumberland Road
    The Erie Canal
      Links between West and East
    The rivalry among Eastern states "   "   IX
      The contest of canals
        The advantage of New York
        The enterprise of Pennsylvania
        The effort of Maryland
      The effect upon the competing cities:
      New York, Philadelphia, and Baltimore
    The transition to railroads   Volume 21, Pages 147–153
  Transportation on the Great Lakes "   Chapter X
    The first cargo carriers
    Canals to connect with world markets
      The activity of Ohio
        Lake Erie to the Ohio River
      Canadian competition
        The Welland canal
        The rivalry of the Hudson and the Saint Lawrence
  The call of the Mississippi
    The portage to Lake Michigan

Inland Transportation—Continued
>   The canal
>   The rise of Chicago
> The opening of the Lake Superior region
>   Copper and iron ore
>   Wheat, corn, and oats
>   Outlet through the Saint Mary's River Ship Canal
> The rapid improvement of ships and harbors
> The steamboat on western rivers   Volume 21, Chapter XI
>   Shreve's river craft
> The peculiarities of the Mississippi
>   The skill of the river pilot
> The heyday of the river trade
>   The servants of King Cotton
>   The luxuries of river travel
>   Rival packet lines
>   Races on the Mississippi
> The gateway of Saint Louis
>   Trade with the South
>   Outlet for the traffic on the Missouri
>   Commerce over the Santa Fé and Oregon Trails
>   The overland route to Salt Lake
>   The Pony Express

The Cotton Gin and the Spread of Cotton Culture
>   Volume 37, Chapter II

> Difficulties of large production
>   Eli Whitney's invention
>   Infringers of his patent
> The enormous increase of production Volume 35, Pages 52–53
>   The spread to upland fields
> The advance of the Old South into the Gulf region
>   The increased value of slaves
>   The extension of the slave system
>   "A positive good"   Volume 27, Chapter III

The Rise of Manufacturing
> The cotton mills of New England   Volume 37, Chapter IV
>   Slater and spinning machinery

The Rise of Manufacturing—Continued
    Lowell and the power loom
        The first mill at Waltham, Massachusetts, 1814
        The founding of Lowell
        An industrial city
        Conditions of labor
    The invention of the sewing machine
        The career of Elias Howe
        Singer and organization
          The beginnings of shoe machinery
    Manufacturing in the South   Volume 27, Pages 44-47
    The development of farm machinery   Volume 37, Chapter V
        The evolution of the plough
        John Deere
        James Oliver
        Grain drills
        The McCormick reaper
          Sales organization   Volume 39, Chapter VI
        The thresher
    The rubber industry   Volume 37, Chapter VII
        The career of Goodyear
        The process of vulcanizing
    Contributions of the American machine-shop
                        Volume 37, Chapter VIII
        John Stevens, pioneer
        Devices for railroads and steamboats
        Eli Whitney's gun parts
          Interchangeability
        Machine tools
        Colt's revolver
          The impress of American methods on Great Britain
    A view of American economic development at the open-
      ing of the Civil War   Volume 37, Pages 123-127

American Labor
    European antecedents   Volume 40, Chapter I
    American differences
        The stream of immigration

American Labor—Continued

      Irish   Volume 35, Chapter V

      German   "   " VI

      Negro labor   "   " III

      The opportunity of the frontier

Beginnings of collective feeling   Volume 40, Pages 21–40

    Early strikes

    The demand for a ten-hour day

      Fuel for the Democratic party

      Cries against the aristocracy

Conditions in the mills of Lowell Volume 37, Pages 93–96

    Observations of Charles Dickens

    A contrasting picture   Volume 40, Page 45

Changes following the panic of 1837 Volume 40, Chapter III

    The effect of the panic

    Humanitarian experiments

    The revival of the labor movement

      Attempts at co-operative production

      Strikes

      The ten-hour day

        Social recognition

    Development of unions

      Extension to women

      The rapid rise of living costs

        Labor's demand for compensation

    The development of labor law

The First American Tariffs

    A safeguard for the new government Volume 14, Pages 26–31

      Source of revenue

        Incidental protection

    The troublous times of Jefferson Volume 15, Chapters VIII–XI

      Non-intercourse

      Embargo

      War

        Stimulation of American industry Volume 37, Pages 88–91

    The advent of peace

      Danger to American manufactures

        The dumping of British goods

The First American Tariffs—Continued
    The tariff of 1816
      A check on British importation
      Protection as the primary purpose
        Nationalist enthusiasm
          Calhoun
        Sectional opposition
          Webster and New England shipowners

The hard times of 1819. With the return of peace after the War of 1812, the United States entered a period of rapid development. The industries which had started under the protection of war counted upon the Tariff of 1816 to give them continued security against foreign manufactures. New settlers hurried to the western territories and bought large tracts of the public land. To finance the first payments on their homesteads, they borrowed from the small banks which sprang up in every locality like mushrooms. The American people were thrilled with the prospect of great wealth in the near future. But the development had been too rapid. Investments in land had gone beyond the possibility of immediate returns into speculation on future values. Banking became a craze. Sound principles were cast aside for "wildcat" schemes. The tariff of 1816 did not hold back the flood of British goods. They were poured upon the American market at such low prices that American industry could not compete. When therefore the Bank of the United States abandoned its policy of expansion, contracted its loans, and forced local banks to liquidate their debts, it precipitated a panic. The hollow structure of prosperity collapsed.

State legislatures and Congress at once sought remedies for the nation-wide distress. State laws placed taxes upon the Bank of the United States in retaliation for its coercion of local banks. Other legislation relieved debtors from immediate payment of their obligations. Congress revised the national land laws. The Act of 1820 reduced the price of public lands from $2.00 to $1.25 an acre, cut down the required amount of purchase from 160 to 80 acres, and abolished the credit system of sales. The Act of 1821 released those who had begun to purchase lands on partial payments from their contracts and gave

to them as much land as they had paid for. Then, Congress raised the tariff duties to protect American industry. Henry Clay championed the Tariff of 1820 and enunciated the principles of his "American System." Protective tariffs were necessary to assure a home market for American manufactures. The industrial states in the east should devote their energy to manufacturing, and the agricultural states in the west would supply them with foodstuffs in return for their manufactures. To bring about such co-operation and independence of foreign goods, Clay insisted that the two sections must be linked with turnpikes and canals, internal improvements. Further, the government should sell the western lands liberally to encourage agriculture. The "American System" had the appearance of a national policy. In reality, it was the program of a sectional alliance. The shipowners of the seaboard and the cotton-planters of the south drew together in opposition and demanded free-trade. The debate over succeeding tariffs revealed an increasingly bitter competition among sectional interests.

Competing sectional interests
    The American System   Volume 19, Pages 178–179
        The demands of Clay for the West   Volume 40, Page 27
    The tariff of 1824   Volume 20, Pages 158–160
        The compromise of the sections
           Opponents of protection
               Webster for the shipowners of New England
               Hayne for the planters of the South

The Tariff of 1824 did not satisfy the producers of woolen goods. England reduced its tax on wool, making it possible for English manufacturers to lower prices and slip their goods into the American market at lower valuations, thus escaping the American duties which were levied *ad valorem*. In 1827 Mallory, a representative in Congress for the wool-growing state of Vermont, introduced a bill which proposed to tax woolen goods according to minimum valuations. Any article valued under the minimum in its class was taxed at that minimum rate. The bill was defeated in the Senate by the vote of Vice-President

Calhoun. Immediately the friends of protection rallied in convention at Harrisburg, Pennsylvania, to frame a program for national action. The presidential candidates of 1828 found that they must state their views. Adams was an outspoken protectionist. Jackson also committed himself to protection, with reservations. But Calhoun and the Southern opponents of protection seemed to count upon bringing Jackson over to their side, and they hoped to make the "Tariff of Abominations" too much for the stomach of New England.

The tariff of 1828
    Reconsideration of the problem   Pages 160–169
    The intervening actions of Great Britain
      Mallory's bill of 1827
    The Harrisburg Convention
      Pressure upon Jackson
      His uncertainty
    The "Tariff of Abominations"
    Southern plans   Volume 27, Page 12
    Acceptance by New England
      The changed opinion of Webster
      The dismay of the South
    Southern remonstrance
      The South Carolina *Exposition*, Dec. 19, 1828
        Calhoun, secret author
    Southern disappointment in Jackson
Fixation of the principle of protection
                Volume 20, Pages 169–178

  The tariff of 1832
    Revision of the duties
      Reduction of revenue
    The determination of South Carolina to oppose
      the principle
    Nullification
Peacemakers
    The failure of Van Buren's friends
      The Verplanck bill
    The success of Clay
The Compromise of 1833   Pages 179–180

The First American Tariffs—Continued
    A sliding scale of duties until 1842
        Protection subordinated to internal peace
    Resumption of the demand for protection in 1842
      Clay and the Whigs against President Tyler
    Return of the Democrats to power
      The Walker tariff, 1846
        Reduction of duties
    The tariff of 1857
      The lowest point of protection
      The panic of 1857   Volume 40, Pages 61–62
        The effect on King Cotton
    The Morrill tariff of 1861   Volume 29, Pages 77, 96
      Campaign promises of the Republicans
      Return to the protective principle

CHAPTER XII

THE NATIONAL BANK, FINANCE, AND THE EARLY
RAILROADS

ON the eve of the second war with England, the
Jeffersonian Republicans had discarded the first
National Bank, which had been organized by the
Federalist Hamilton. As a result, their government had to fight without adequate means to
handle the financial problems that the war created.
They tried to employ state banks as their fiscal
agents. Chaos was inevitable. One of the first
of the post-war problems, accordingly, was the
establishment of a new national bank, the second
Bank of the United States, modeled closely upon
Hamilton's institution. Upon the return of peace,
a craze for banking swept over the country with
the wave of national enthusiasm. Speculation in
western lands enticed local banks into unsound
investments. Even the new Bank of the United
States was led into the speculative dance for a

time, but it soon abandoned such a dangerous
policy and set itself to conduct a conservative
business and serve the nation. Its size and power,
and its resistance to wildcat banking, brought upon
it the hostility of the frontier people. When
Jackson, representative of the West, came to the
presidency, those western prejudices against aristocracy and privileged classes turned him against
the Bank. He opposed its re-charter and took
the national revenues from its control to deposit
them with "pet banks." The Panic of 1837, in
part a result of Jackson's actions, left a majority
of the American people convinced that private
institutions should not be allowed to handle public
funds. Jackson's successor, Martin Van Buren,
proposed the Independent Treasury to care for
the government's money.

In the year of Jackson's election to the presidency the first railroad across the Appalachian
mountains was begun. Yet it was not until the
Forties that the new means of transportation began to come into its own. The canal boom had
lasted from the completion of the successful Erie
Canal in 1825 to the Panic of 1837. When prosperity came again it was the railroad rather than
the tow-path that held public attention. A na-

tional system of communications spread an ever increasing web of tracks over the country from the Atlantic coast to the Mississippi. With the discovery of gold in California transcontinental lines were talked of. In this expansion, the North far outstripped the South until the railroad had bound New England more closely to the Northwest than in a previous decade the Mississippi river had joined it to the South.

But the growth was too rapid for a new country. A temporary check came in the Panic of 1857 which brought distress and heavy losses to Northern industry and agriculture. King Cotton, however, escaped, and the Southerners reasoned that their section was economically unassailable. Disillusionment did not come to them until four years later, when the superior industrial and transportation facilities of the North told heavily in the war between the states. To the Confederacy, the war brought social and economic ruin. The North, though slowed down, continued to make economic progress.

The Story of the Bank of the United States
   Origin   Volume 16, Pages 124–126
   Early management   Volume 20, Pages 181–183
     The share in the crisis of 1819

The Story of the Bank of the United States—Continued
  The changed policy
    The pressure on speculative enterprises
    The enmity of democratic elements   Volume 19, Page 179
      States rights
          McCulloch versus Maryland Volume 16, Pages 126–135
          Osborn versus The United States Bank
                                  Volume 16, Pages 189–190
  Its course during the twenties   Volume 20, Pages 183–198
    Nicholas Biddle
    The charges of the Democrats
      Political directors
      The Portsmouth affair
        Influence on Jackson
          His message to Congress
  Jackson's war on the Bank
    Biddle's lobby for re-charter
    Jackson's veto of the bill
      The election of 1832   Volume 40, Page 27
    "Removal of the Deposits"
    The use of "Pet Banks"
      The temptation to speculate

The Panic of 1837   Volume 20, Pages 199–200

The causes which have thrown the American people into financial panics have moved in cycles. The underlying forces of the panic of 1819 slowly regained control over the mind of the public and plunged it to disaster again in 1837. Stimulated by a succession of good years, the American people once more became over sanguine. They built canals and railroads beyond the needs of the country. Their state governments borrowed heavily of British capital for internal improvements. They embarked in wild banking enterprises and speculated feverishly in cotton plantations, city real estate, and western lands. A vicious circle was soon in operation piling up unsound credit accounts in local banks. For these loans, the banks issued in large part their own paper currency. The borrowers presented the bank notes at the public land office in payment for their purchases. The land office deposited the bank notes as national

revenues in the local "pet bank" of Jackson's administration. With these additional funds at its disposal, the bank proceeded to make further loans of paper money. In this round of transactions nothing of intrinsic worth had changed hands except the land, and it was, too frequently, uncultivated or non-productive. Crop failures, furthermore, delayed returns from the investments in land and obliged the banks to carry the accounts of their creditors longer than they had planned. As a result, they were rapidly approaching the brink of disaster when Jackson's "Specie Circular" required that payments for public lands be made in gold or silver coin. Then, the tower of credit tumbled suddenly in ruins. To make matters worse for the government, it had begun, at the insistence of Clay and his followers, to distribute among the states the surplus which had been accumulating in the national treasury since the national debt had been extinguished in 1835.

The panic of 1837, however, was not entirely due to the faults of the American people. In fact, it was precipitated by failures in Great Britain. The excess of British exports to the United States during the Thirties had been balanced by the sale of American securities in Great Britain and the establishment of credits abroad. Large commercial houses in London with close American relations were affected by these failures and obliged to contract their credits. American business at once was sharply depressed.

Overaction
  Banking
  Canals   Compare Volume 21, Chapter IX
  Railroad building   Volume 38, Pages 9–10
The vicious circle
  The sale of lands
  The "Specie Circular"
The distribution of the surplus
The effects of the crash
  Political   Volume 24, Pages 102, 121
    Texas
  Social   Volume 40, Pages 34–35, 40, 50–51
    Labor

The Panic of 1837—Continued
    Economic   Volume 38, Pages 47, 68, 100
      Business   Volume 37, Pages 99, 141
    Financial   Volume 20, Page 199
      The national treasury

The Sub-Treasury System   Volume 20, Pages 199–200
  Van Buren's remedy
    The recognized failure of the pet banks
    The Democratic refusal to restore the Bank of the
      United States
    A national system of vaults in central cities
      The protection of national revenues
      The circulation of Treasury notes
  The fight for the new system
  Success in 1840
  Repeal by the Whigs
    Tyler and Clay
  Restoration by the Democrats
    Polk
  Retention until modified during the Civil War
    Chase's system of national depositories
                       Volume 29, Page 200

The Improvement of Communications
  The railroad
    The inventors   Volume 37, Pages 69–83
      The Americans, Evans and Stevens
      The Englishman, Stephenson
      Peter Cooper and the *Tom Thumb*
    The transition from canals to railroads
                 Volume 21, Pages 147–153
                 Volume 37, Page 80
                 Volume 38, Pages 1–13
                 Volume 35, Pages 110–113
    The Baltimore and Ohio   Volume 38, Pages 95–102
    The Pennsylvania   "   "   Pages 47–49
    The New York Central   "   "   Pages 20–29
    The Erie   "   "   Pages 64–71

The Improvement of Communications—Continued

  Early railroads in the South

    The Charleston and Hamburg   Volume 38, Page 10

      Augusta, Georgia   Volume 37, Page 80

    The cotton belt roads   Volume 27, Pages 36–37

    The project of a road to the Pacific

                      Volume 27, Pages 131–132

  The transcontinental line

  The ever widening horizon of the West

    The pathway of the Lakes   Volume 21, Pages 170–173

    Trail heads on the plains   Pages 190–195

  The startling effect of gold in California

                    Volume 38, Pages 120–123

    Surveys, 1853

    The Union Pacific Act, 1862

    The Santa Fé route   "   "   Page 154

  The Telegraph   Volume 37, Chapter VI

  Morse's invention

  The demonstration from Washington to Baltimore

  Use by the Democratic convention, 1844

  Extension around the world

  Across the continent, 1862

    The end of the Pony Express

  Under the Atlantic

    The first cable, 1868

The Panic of 1857   Volume 40, Pages 61–62

  Collapse due to overdevelopment of railroads

              Volume 38, Pages 13, 26, 101

  An industrial crisis   Volume 36, Pages 176–177

  Injury to the western farmers

  The escape of Cotton

CHAPTER XIII

APPROPRIATION OF THE CONTINENT

AMERICA was not to be held within the bounds of the inheritance from Great Britain or the purchase from France. It was to acquire more and more territory and constantly to advance its frontier westward. In the Twenties the Floridas finally fell from the weak grasp of Spain. In the Thirties Americans laid out their plantations on the Texan plains within the domain of Mexico. They revolted against the control of a people to whom they were foreign in blood and tradition and won their independence on the battlefield. During the Forties, long trains of canvas-covered prairie schooners jolted over the Oregon Trail to the valley of the Columbia. Oregon, hitherto a fur-trading country, the home of a handful of British and American trappers and traders, became an American settlement. In 1844, complete ownership was demanded by the people of the United

States. Two years later England consented to divide the region at the forty-ninth parallel. In the same year war broke out between the United States and Mexico, incensed over the American annexation of Texas. The treaty of peace which brought an end to the conflict added the vast region of Arizona, New Mexico, and California to the territory of the United States. Throughout these decades, Americans had talked much of their country's "manifest destiny" to possess the continent from sea to sea. By 1848 this ambition had become a reality. Immediately after the Civil War the Russian offer to sell Alaska was accepted.

The peace treaty with Mexico had hardly been signed when gold was discovered in California. The Mormons, who had journeyed over the first mountain barrier into the arid valleys of Utah to establish their own independent state, as they thought, far beyond the reach of the United States, now saw the tide of American migration rush past them to the gold fields. A large American settlement at once appeared in the great central valley of California. The earlier Spanish traditions and civilization were submerged. When gold mining became less profitable, farming took its place. The new community did not break up. The early

Americans in California were not daunted by the problems of a rapidly increasing population. They brought order out of lawlessness in a way that reveals fundamental qualities in the American character.

"Manifest Destiny" had carried the border of the United States to the Pacific. But the frontier did not sweep westward in an uninterrupted course across the continent following the acquisition of new lands. It pushed up the western slope of the Mississippi Valley approximately to the region of the High Plains; then it leaped the barrier of the Rockies and the Sierra Nevadas and appeared in the valleys of the Pacific coast. The settlement of the region of the mountains and the High Plains was delayed until after the war between the states. This was the last American frontier.

Early in our history the original English-speaking stock, always in the forefront of westward expansion, had been joined by newcomers from Europe, who were attracted by the cheap lands. Germans, Irish, and Swedes were the most numerous. The negro, held fast by slavery, was seldom found north of the cotton-producing areas of the West. As, year after year, the stream of settlement moved on, gaining steadily in volume, it

worked prodigious changes. Early pack trails gave way to roads and railroads. Mountain prospectors, picturesque seekers after the golden fleece, were supplanted by the capitalist and the mining corporation. The vast herds of bison that roamed the grasslands east of the Rockies melted away leaving the Indians of the plains deprived of the very foundation of their life. War flamed up from Dakota to Texas, the last desperate stand of a doomed race. Herds of cattle succeeded the bison. Then the cattleman had to abandon his ranges to the farmer enclosing his little homestead with barbed wire fences. With the advent of the plough, the frontier passed rapidly out of American life.

The settlers who broke the virgin soil and set themselves to the task of making homes on the western plains had naturally a zeal for education. To support it a fine missionary spirit in the older communities along the Atlantic seaboard sent money for the endowment of schools and colleges. They were almost without exception religious institutions, sometimes perhaps established to do little more than propagate particular sectarian convictions among the folk of the frontier, but more often imbued with a spirit of genuine service.

As the West grew in population and prosperity the idea that education was a public concern became practically universal. From it sprang to vigorous life those state universities that are typical of America west of the Appalachians.

The Acquisition of the Floridas   Volume 15, Chapter V
  West Florida
    The revolt of the inhabitants   Pages 189–198
    The annexation by the United States
  East Florida   XIII
    Spanish rule
    Refuge for enemies of the United States
    American ambitions
    Jackson's punitive expedition
    The Florida treaty with Spain
      Definition of the southwestern boundary

The Story of Oregon   Volume 22, Chapters I–VII
  Rival claims
    Explorers, Lewis and Clark
    Traders, Astoria
  Diplomacy
    The convention of 1818 with Great Britain
         Volume 15, Pages 293–294
    The treaty with Spain   Pages 282–283
    The convention with Russia   Pages 303–304
  The race for settlement   Volume 22, Chapter VIII
    Marcus Whitman
  The treaty with England of 1846   "   "   Pages 263–266

The Story of Texas   Volume 24, Chapters I, II
  The Mexican revolution
  American migration into Texas
    The Mexican colonization law
    The prohibition of slavery
  The Texan war for independence   "   "   III
    Edwards, Austin, Houston

The Story of Texas—Continued
    The Alamo   Volume 24, Chapter IV
    San Jacinto
    The Republic of Texas   "   "   V–VII
    Negotiations with the United States for annexation

The Mexican War
    Mexican suspicions of the United States
        Commodore Jones at Monterey   Volume 24, Page 115
        The annexation of Texas   "   "   VIII–X
            British interests
            The question of slavery
        The Slidell mission   "   "   X
    American military operations
        Polk's message
        The invasion of Mexico   XI, XII, XIII
            Taylor
            Scott
        The treaty of Guadaloupe-Hidalgo   "   "   XIV

The Trek of the Mormons   Volume 25, Chapter VI
    Beginnings in New York, Ohio, Missouri, and Illinois
    The state of Deseret
        Salt Lake City

The Rush for Gold   Volume 25, Chapters I–IV
    Early American settlements in California
    The Forty-niners
        Across the plains   Volume 25, Chapter V
        By way of Panama   "   "   VII
        The diggings   "   "   VIII

The American Occupation of California   "   "   IX–XV
    San Francisco
    The Vigilantes

The Purchase of Alaska   Volume 46, Chapter III
    The Russian offer
    Seward's eagerness
    The bargain

Immigration and Western Settlement
  The original stock   Volume 35, Chapters I, II
  Americans and negroes   "   "   III
    The slave system
    The freedman
  Americans and seekers after Utopia   "   "   IV
  Americans and foreigners
    The Irish   "   "   V
    The Germans   "   "   VI
    Swedes and others
  The lure of the West   "   "   VII
    Cheap land

The Passing of the Frontier   Volume 26, Chapters I–VI
  Early trails
  Prospectors and miners
  Cowboys and cattle trails
  The Indian wars   "   "   VII
  Cattle kings   "   "   VIII
  The homesteader   "   "   IX

The Westward Movement of Education   Volume 33, Chapter XI
  The rivalry of sectarians
    Contests for college sites
    Eastern philanthropy
  Endowment by land grant
    The eccentricities of legislatures
  State Universities   "   "   XII
    French and German influences
    The model, Michigan University

CHAPTER XIV

SIDE by side with expansion to the Pacific coast during the first half of the Nineteenth Century went the growth of sectional dissension within the nation. The trouble arose from contrasts between the North and South that were, in the last analysis, the outgrowth of a climatic difference. North of the Ohio were the varied conditions of the temperate zone. To the south of it, the climate became more and more subtropical. In the heart of the cotton and sugar country white men could not work efficiently at manual labor. To supply the necessary labor, negroes had been imported from Africa early in colonial times. It was found that in the South, whether the crop was tobacco, rice, or cotton, negroes could be used most efficiently when handled in gangs. This led to the growth of the plantation system. Its growth was further stimulated by the cheapness

of land in the new country and by the need for constant substitution of virgin soil in place of fields worn out by cropping. When the invention of the cotton-gin, in 1793, fixed cotton as the staple crop of the South, the plantation system with its slave labor was firmly established and practically universalized. The only areas into which it did not advance were the upland valleys of the Appalachians and the lowland regions where the soil was sandy and infertile.

The plantation brought about a definite and permanent social stratification. At the top was the planter and at the bottom the slave. Between the two were grades of lesser whites and free blacks. The southern civilization was aristocratic to the core. Its outstanding characteristics were differences in wealth, social position, and political power.

In sharp contrast was the democracy of the Northwest, built also upon agriculture. The small farmer of the northern half of the Ohio valley was the economic and political equal of his neighbor. In the communities where he lived, democracy was as inevitable as cultivating the land. Here slave labor was economically so inefficient that the prohibition of the Ordinance of 1787 was hardly needed. In the northern states, east of

the Alleghanies, commercial and industrial enterprises were rapidly developing. But, although they were causing an unequal distribution of wealth, they were not as yet seriously modifying the general ideal of democracy.

In the young United States, therefore, two civilizations had appeared: one agricultural, commercial and industrial, with its political institutions founded on democracy; the other almost solely agricultural, with its social and political life built on aristocracy. Both civilizations, in the beginning, supported the central government and favored national expansion.

Three factors made for discord. The first was the inevitable dislike of the people of each section for the different institutions and ideals of the other. This was particularly true in the North where the dislike of slavery grew to the proportions of a moral crusade. The second was a disparity in growth of population, a condition which threatened the equality of the South with the North in the councils of the nation. This led to the development of an interpretation of the Constitution to protect the rights of a minority, the theory of nullification. The third and probably the most important factor was the competition of the two

civilizations for the unsettled public domain. Northerners, naturally, wished to exclude the obnoxious institution of slavery from the new country. Southerners, quite as naturally, wished to increase the area of their section as much as possible. They were anxious to expand into the territories of Texas and California. The sectional struggle became most acute on the climatic borderline where the states of Missouri and Kansas were established. This struggle for the national domain ultimately brought on war.

It is perhaps easier to understand why the South wished to abandon the Union than why the North desired to compel it to stay. The Southerner who squarely faced the facts saw clearly that his civilization was menaced; that the North wished to and was able to put slavery on the way to ultimate extinction. He believed that the result in his own section would be a social revolution, the consequences of which no man could foresee. His home, his wife and daughters, the whole structure of his society would be confronted by a black menace if the slaves should gain their freedom and feel the power that lay in their numbers. If this was the price that he must pay for loyalty to the Union, he would fight, if need be, for Southern

freedom. Why, he asked, if the Northerner so deeply disliked Southern institutions, should the North not be willing to let the South go in peace? Why undertake a fratricidal war to compel an unwilling section to remain within a Union that threatened to tear in shreds its whole social fabric?

The answer is not easy. In the North, as the country had expanded, the spirit of nationalism had grown. Webster had preached it in his great orations; Clay had woven it into the compromises with which he was associated; economic interchange had knit the nation into a closer and closer union. If the South left the Union the nation would be deeply, irreparably wounded. Was such to be the ending to the dreams of the men who had labored to make America free and to establish its independence? Northerners, already angered at the South for wrongs that they believed the "slaveocracy" had committed, could not stand calmly by and permit this colossal injury to their nation. National patriotism was, therefore, enlisted against the Southerner. Many men in the North joined the Union armies to free the black man. The battle was joined with idealism burning bright on both sides. The time of America's greatest testing was at hand.

The Early Slave Question
The negro   Volume 9, Pages 194–203
                                Volume 35, Chapter III
  Ordeals of the slave trade   "   " Pages 45–52
  Colonial slave codes
    The decline of slavery
  The spirit of freedom
    The Revolution   Volume 28, Chapter I
      The Ordinance of 1787   Volume 13, Pages 76–79
    Constitutional conservatism
      The slave trade   Pages 129–130
 Geographical rifts   Volume 28, Chapter II
  The abolition of slavery in the North
  The spread of cotton raising in the South
                    Compare Volume 35, Pages 52–56
    The place of the negro Compare Volume 37, Pages 50–51
    Evasions of the law against the African slave trade
    The competition for new states

The Missouri Compromise   Volume 15, Pages 309–310
  The application for admission, 1819
    Debates in Congress   Volume 28, Pages 16–18
  The application of Maine   Volume 16, Page 127
    The balance maintained

The Crusade against Slavery   Volume 28, Chapter III
  The pioneers
    The Quaker Lundy
      His opinion of removal to Africa
      Zeal for emancipation
      His newspaper
    The Puritan Garrison
      Vehemence for immediate emancipation
        The Liberator
    The slaveholder Birney
      Gradual emancipation
        His appeal to fellow Southerners
      Labors for the colonization society
      The displeasure of his neighbors
      A leader of the political abolitionists

The Crusade against Slavery—Continued
        Friction with Garrison
     Feminine agitators
      The sisters Grimke
        Carolinians
        The evangelist spirit
          The Quaker garb
      Parallel campaigns for the emancipation of woman,
        temperance, and the abolition of war
     Oberlin College
      Higher education for negroes
     The Abolition Spirit in the West
The turning-point   Volume 28, Chapter IV
     Garrison's *Address to the Public*, 1831
     Nat Turner's insurrection
      Southern fear and fury
     Grave debates in the legislature of Virginia
      The effect of British emancipation, 1833
        Heightened Southern consciousness
Array for battle   Volume 28, Chapter V
     Abolitionists: liberators or incendiaries
      The resistance of conservatives, Northern and
          Southern
        Restrictions on the black man's privileges
        The attack upon Garrison in Boston, 1835
        The persecution of Miss Crandall in Connecticut
        The death of Lovejoy in Illinois, 1837
        Southern petitions to Northern legislatures
        The pressure upon religion
          The split of the churches   Volume 28, Page 84
      Anti-slavery literature in the mails
        Bonfires in the South
        The attitude of Jackson's administration
          Amos Kendall
          Jackson's attack on the abolitionists
        The victory of Anti-slavery

The Fight over the "Gag Rule"   Volume 28, Pages 78–84
     Abolitionist petitions in Congress

The Fight over the " Gag Rule"—Continued
    Southern insistence upon the "gag rule"
  The ire of J. Q. Adams
    Champion of the right of petition
      His excoriation of Southern Congressmen
  Giddings and freedom of debate
    The Creole affair, 1841

The Cotton Kingdom   Volume 27, Chapter I
  The lower South
    Its climate and soil
    The spread of cotton
      The removal of the Indians
      The planter upon the heels of the pioneer
        The increase of slave holding
    Social groups
      French culture centered in New Orleans
        The Catholic Church
      The society of Charleston
        The vanishing English gentry
        French Huguenots
      The poor folk of the hills
        Their religion
        Their rise to the planter class
  The development of an aristocracy of planters
                     Volume 27, Chapter II
    The rising price of cotton
      The increasing value of slaves
    Dependence upon the North for manufactures
      Obligations to Northern bankers
      Northern profits in slavery
    Subordinate lower classes
      Small farmers
      Tenants
      "Piney woods" squatters
      "Crackers"
        Contempt for the negro
    The independent Southern class
      The mountaineers

The Cotton Kingdom—Continued
  Their isolation from the Cotton Kingdom
The cotton belt
  Its railroad connections with the seaboard
    Ties with the tobacco areas
The slave traders
  Trade between the Old South and the New
Growing sectional consciousness
  Trade with the Northwest
  Investments of Eastern capital
  The exhaustion of the soil
    The demand for new lands to the South and West
    A future in manufacturing
      Water power
      Cheap negro labor
      "Manifest Destiny"
        Cuba, Mexico, and Central America
Planter philosophy   Volume 27, Chapter III
  The place of the poor white
    The decline of Jeffersonian dogma
      The work of Dew
      The finishing touch by Harper
  Calhoun's announcement
    Slavery, a positive good
  The chivalry of the South
    The mirror of Scott's novels
    Justification in Carlyle
    Support by Christianity
  Protestors
    Goodlow
    Helper
    Weston
Southern Society   Volume 27, Chapter IV
  The plantation
    The house
    The negro quarters
  Dress and social customs
    Saratoga and Washington
    The Battery at Charleston

The Cotton Kingdom—Continued
 Southern libraries
  Newspapers and reviews
  Congressional records
  Scott, Byron, and Thackeray
  The dislike of Dickens
  Dr. Johnson and Goldsmith
  Shakespeare
   The theater
  Greek and Latin
   "Log colleges"
 Southern poets and authors
  Followers of the English tradition
   Simms, Kennedy, Timrod, Hayne
  Portraitists of the South
   Longstreet, Thompson, Hooper, Baldwin
    The Southern Literary Messenger
 The life of the poor whites
  Log house, negro cabin, and barn
  Dwellers on the pine barrens
  Poverty and illiteracy
 Religion and education   Volume 27, Chapter V
  The deism of Cooper and Jefferson
  The path of orthodoxy
   Fashionable Episcopalians
   Missionary Presbyterians
    The faith of Calvin
    War upon the deists
   Ardent Methodists and Baptists
  The transformation of the South
   Acceptance of slavery by the evangelistic sects
    Division of the Methodist and Baptist churches
     North and South
    Strife in the Presbyterian national organization
  The growth of education
   Increased attendance in the colleges
   Famous teachers
   Scientific research
   Improvement of common schools

The Cotton Kingdom—Continued
  The blight of illiteracy
  Instruction for negroes

The Flower of American Literature
 The New England school of philosophers
          Volume 34, Chapter VI

  The new liberalism
   W. E. Channing
   Emerson
   Thoreau
    Hatred of slavery
  Romancers and poets   " "   VII
   Hawthorne
   Longfellow
   Whittier
    Abolitionist
  Wits and satirists
   Holmes
   Lowell
    The Biglow papers
  Historians
   Sparks and Bancroft
   Prescott, Motley, and Parkman
  Poe and Whitman   " "   VIII

The Question of Slavery in New Territories
          Volume 28, Chapter VI
          Volume 27, Chapter VI
  Texas   Volume 24, Pages 90–109
  The growth of Anti-slavery
  J. Q. Adams in Congress
  The recognition of the Texan Republic
   The effect of the murder of the Abolitionist
    Lovejoy
   The birth of the Liberty Party
    The election of 1840
  The fight over the annexation of Texas
        Volume 24, Chapters VIII, IX

The Question of Slavery in New Territories—Continued
    The election of 1844
      The southern abandonment of Van Buren
      The failure of Clay for the Whigs
      Election of the western Democrat, Polk
Spoils of the Mexican War   Volume 24, Chapter X
   The dreams of an expansionist President
   Justification for war on Mexico
     American claims
   The opposition
   Conscience Whigs
   Barnburner Democrats
    Van Buren
   The Wilmot Proviso   Volume 28, Page 91
                        Volume 27, Page 125

California and New Mexico
   Free soil or slave?
    The election of 1848
      Cass for Democrats
      Van Buren for Free Soilers
      Taylor for Whigs
       The success of the Whigs
The Compromise of 1850   Volume 28, Chapter VII
   The refractoriness of Taylor
   Resistance to encroachment from any quarter
   Incipient Southern defiance
    The Nashville Convention   Volume 27, Pages 126–127
   Clay's proposals for compromise
   The death of Taylor
   The acceptance of the Compromise
    The death-knell of the Whig party

Irreconcilable Elements of Discord
   Northern opposition to the Fugitive Slave Law
    The election of 1852   Volume 27, Pages 127–128
                        Volume 28, Page 144
      The issue: Finality of the Compromise
      Democratic acceptance

Irreconcilable Elements of Discord—Continued
       Free Soil opposition
       Whig neutrality
     The Democratic victory
     The death of the Whig party
   Increasing assistance for escaping slaves
                       Volume 28, Chapter VIII

     Rescues
       Shadrach and Jerry
       The Burns affair   Compare Volume 29, Page 27
     The roads to Canada
     Mountain refugees
   The spur of *Uncle Tom's Cabin*   Volume 28, Chapter IX
     The experience of Mrs. Stowe Volume 34, Pages 220–223
     The effect upon the youth of America
     The influence in Europe
Southern determination to dominate or secede
   Control of the national government Volume 27, Pages 128–137
     President Pierce
   Southern expansion
     The Gadsden Purchase
     The Ostend Manifesto
The dual nation   Volume 29, Chapter I
The statesmanship of Douglas
   A scheme for escape from the dilemma
     The Kansas-Nebraska Bill   Volume 29, Pages 15–18
                      Volume 28, Chapter X
       The mixed motives of Douglas   Volume 27, Page 132
                      Volume 29, Chapter II
       Promotion of a northern railroad to the Pacific
       Surrender to the "Slave Power"
       Adherence to the tradition of Jacksonian
         Democracy
        Popular Sovereignty
     The supersession of the Missouri Compromise
      (1820) by the Compromise of 1850
The struggle for Kansas   Volume 28, Chapter X
   Northern indignation with Douglas
     The Emigrant Aid Company

Irreconcilable Elements of Discord—Continued
 Border ruffians from Missouri
  A bowie-knife and pistol election
  Support by President Pierce
   The removal of Governor Reeder
   The appointment of Shannon
  The free-state convention
   The Topeka Constitution
   The election of Governor Robinson
 The rival governments
  The Wakarusa War
  Buford's troop from Alabama
  "Beecher's Bibles" from Connecticut
 Civil War in Kansas
  The sack of Lawrence
  John Brown's message from God
 The efforts of Governor Geary to re-establish order
  His resignation in disgust
   The failure of Pierce to give support

The Rise of the Republican Party   Volume 29, Chapter II
 Anti-Nebraska men   Volume 43, Pages 13–14
 The transitory Know-Nothing Party
  Hostility to the foreigner
  A temporary refuge for old Whigs
 The Free Soil remnant
 The effect of the struggle for Kansas
  Stimulation of sectional patriotism in the North
   The fusion of anti-slavery elements
    The birth of the Republican party
   Seward's adherence to the new cause
   The election of Banks as Speaker of the House, 1856
 The election of 1856   Volume 28, Pages 162–163
           Volume 27, Pages 138–139

 Candidates
  Fremont for Republicans
  Buchanan for Democrats
  Fillmore for Know-Nothings
 The issue: Admission of Kansas under the Topeka

The Rise of the Republican Party—Continued
    Constitution
   The victory of conservatism
   The election of Buchanan

The Growth of the Desire for Separation   Volume 29, Chapter III
                              Volume 27, Pages 139–143
  The ebbing strength of Southern Unionists
  Old Whig leaders
  The rise of the "Fire-Eaters" to power
   Yancey and Rhett
  Southern commercial conventions
   The "Slave Interest"
    Allies in New York
   The demand for reopening the slave trade
    Secession, the alternative
 Sumner, contemptuous and contemptible
                              Volume 28, Chapter XI
  His Free-Soil record
  Blistering arraignments of Southern morals
  "The Crime against Kansas," 1856
   The attack by Butler
  "The Barbarism of Slavery," 1859
 The failure of Buchanan to heal the sore of Kansas
                              Volume 28, Chapter XII
  Governor Walker, Southern Democrat
   Political descendant of Andrew Jackson
  His promise to the people of Kansas
  Election frauds
   Pro-slave control of the constitutional convention
  The Lecompton Constitution
   The evasion of the free-state legislature
   Manipulation of the slavery clauses
  Walker's protest to Buchanan
   The rejection of the Lecompton Constitution by the
    people of Kansas
   Buchanan's determination to support it in Congress
 The national judiciary discredited   Volume 28, Chapter XIII
  The southern character of the Supreme Court

The Growth of the Desire for Separation—Continued

    The Dred Scott decision   Volume 27, Page 140

                                          Volume 29, Pages 50–51

        The Missouri Compromise (1820) declared uncon-
            stitutional

    Northern opinion

    Perversion of the Court by political interests

  The sincerity of Douglas vindicated

    His defense of popular sovereignty

        War upon Buchanan   Volume 29, Page 49

                                      Volume 28, Pages 187–188

                                      Volume 27, Pages 140–141

        The defeat of the Lecompton Constitution

                                      Volume 29, Pages 50–58

        The appeal to the people of the Northwest

                                      Volume 28, Pages 199–202

                                      Volume 27, Page 142

      The Lincoln-Douglas debates

        The Dred Scott decision, a stumbling block

        The Freeport Doctrine

           Slavery dependent upon local legislation

           An impossibility

John Brown, revolutionist   Volume 28, Chapter XIV

  His religious environment

    His sympathy with the black man

      Gileadites

  Bleeding Kansas

  The sword of righteousness

    The attack on Harper's Ferry

      The effect upon the South

      The execution of Brown

The Crisis of 1860   Volume 29, Chapter IV

                                    Volume 27, Pages 143–146

  Forewarning

    The observations of Helper, a Southerner, 1857

                                    Volume 28, Pages 137–143

    The appeal to the middle class of the South

      The blight of slavery

The Crisis of 1860—Continued
    The rage of the planters
        The use of Helper's book by the Republican party
    Demands of the Southern extremists
    The reopening of the slave trade
        The Vicksburg resolution, 1859
    The widening of the split between the Southern factions
        The popularity of American adventurers in Central America
   Southern frenzy over John Brown's raid
    The vision of a slave rebellion
    Deafness to Lincoln's censure of Brown
    "Grim desire for self preservation"
        Violence in Congress
        The resolutions of Jefferson Davis
            Congress must protect slavery against territorial legislatures
  The battle of candidates
   The contest for the nomination of the Democratic party
    The convention at Charleston
        The opposition of the South to Douglas
        The dispute over his platform
            The withdrawal of Yancey
        Rival nominations
            Douglas
            Breckenridge
   The Constitutional Union Party
    The fusion of old Whigs and Know-Nothings
        Candidates
            President — J. Bell of Tennessee
            Vice-President — E. Everett of Massachusetts
    The love of Union and the old order
   The Republican convention at Chicago
    A sectional enthusiasm
        Seward, the man of the hour
    The selection of Lincoln
        The man of destiny

The Crisis of 1860—Continued
    A sectional party
      A *Unionist* leader
    The campaign
      The platform of the Republican party
        Free labor in the territories
          An appeal to old Southern Whigs
        Protective tariffs
          An appeal to manufacturing interests
        Rights of democracy
          An appeal to western prejudices
      The threat of the South
      Secession upon the election of Lincoln
    Lincoln, choice of a minority
      The division of the South

Secession   Volume 29, Chapter V
                                     Volume 30, Chapter I
South Carolina's proud recollection of Nullification
    The first to secede — December 20th
Painful decisions of the leaders
    Buchanan "pale with fear"
      Southern demands for Federal property in the South
      Anderson's garrison at Fort Sumter
        The courage of Jeremiah S. Black
Robert E. Lee   Compare Volume 31, Pages 9–11
The peace party
    Nonresisters
      Wendell Phillips and Horace Greeley
    Compromisers
      Weed and Crittenden
        The line of the Missouri Compromise
      Northern capitalists
        Creditors of the South
          August Belmont
Increasing tension
    The failure of the Crittenden Compromise
      Stipulations of the South
      Lincoln's refusal — December 20th

Secession—Continued
    The *Star of the West*
        The failure of relief for Fort Sumter
   The Southern point of view
    The secession of the Gulf States
        Florida, Georgia, Mississippi, Alabama, Louisiana
        The resignation of Jefferson Davis from the Senate
          of the United States
        The devotion of Samuel Houston to the Union
          His defeat in Texas
    The organization of the Confederacy
        Jefferson Davis, President
    The Republican control of the Congress of the United
        States
        The Morrill Tariff
        The admission of Kansas
          A free state
    The failure of the Peace Convention at Washington
        Ex-President Tyler presiding
    Lincoln's journey to Washington
        Disappointment with his speeches
          "Simple Susan"
        His inaugural address
          No interference with slavery in the states
          Enforcement of the Fugitive Slave Law
          Maintenance of the Union
            A step nearer war
            Support by Douglas

The Literature of Union and Liberty   Volume 34, Chapter IX
   The orators
    Clay and Webster
        Statesmen
    Everett and Choate
        Stylists
    Wendell Phillips
        Zealot
   The Journalists
    Garrison, vituperator

The Literature of Union and Liberty—Continued
    Greeley, spokesman for the plain people
  Uncle Tom's Cabin
    Harriet Beecher Stowe
  Abraham Lincoln

CHAPTER XV

ALL efforts to reconcile the sections were in vain. Southern radicals went defiantly from secession to the organization of a Confederacy. Lincoln refused to accept a compromise which altered the original terms of Union. North and South waited tensely for the overt act that would precipitate war. Southern batteries fired upon Fort Sumter in the harbor of Charleston; there was then no turning back. After the first encounter, each side paused for a time and with feverish haste undertook the organization of its strength. The North was superior in man-power and in economic resources. The South excelled in the initial unity of sentiment among its people and in the caliber of its military leaders. Moreover, its task was easier than that of its opponent. To win, the South had only to hold off the Federal armies until the North grew tired of fighting, or a foreign na-

tion interfered. To that end, Southern agents labored persistently at Paris and London. The North could only secure victory by destroying completely the military power of the South, a task of extreme difficulty.

To the North from the beginning went the offensive. Its strategy was directed toward three objectives: first, to blockade the Southern coast and thus prevent the export of cotton and the import of war materials; second, to open navigation on the Mississippi and thereby isolate the western half of the Confederacy; and third, to capture Richmond, the Southern capital. By 1863, the blockade was working with such efficiency that the South was slowly being strangled. Control of the Mississippi, from source to mouth, was finally secured with the surrender of Vicksburg on July 3, 1863. By November of the same year, practically all of the region west of the Appalachian mountains was cut off from the Confederacy by the Federal victory at Chattanooga. In 1864, while Grant struggled with Lee in the wilderness of Virginia, Sherman drove across the southern end of the Atlantic slope and destroyed the military power of the Lower South. It was in Virginia that Confederate armies made their

magnificent stand.   For four years, they held off
the heaviest Northern attacks and even made two
counter-attacks.   These proved to be without
lasting results, for they failed either to force the
North to give up the war or to secure foreign intervention.   Nevertheless, it was not until practically all of the Confederacy outside of Virginia
had fallen into the hands of the enemy that the
confederate government fled from Richmond and
Lee's army collapsed.   There was no peace treaty.
Southern political and military organization, central and local, had been destroyed.   The military
government of Northern armies took its place.

Strange indeed was the contrast between the two
presidents who directed the warring sections.
Davis was of the aristocracy, with military training and a long political experience.   He was called
to the leadership of a united people, fired with the
conviction that their cause was just.   But during
the term of office he was forced to watch the Confederacy slowly disintegrate and was driven to the
bitter realization that his people had lost confidence in him.   Lee, not Davis, became the sym-
bol of Southern idealism.   Lincoln came from
humble folk.   His education was scanty and his
political experience limited.   At a time of crisis he

was called to the leadership of a people still grop-
ing for a way out of besetting difficulties. He
handled skilfully a group of able subordinates,
often hostile to himself, and he guided the North
far along the road to unity. In his policies a stern
purpose was tempered by humanity. When his
death came, his section almost universally hailed
Lincoln as the saviour of the nation.

The Civil War was a great selective force. The
very fact of the war was, in itself, evidence that
two civilizations, such as were typified in the North
and the South, could not exist side by side in the
nation. The war selected out one of these, the
southern, and destroyed it. After the conflict
ended, vindictive elements in the North gained
the ascendency at the national capital and forced
a pitiless course of reconstruction upon the former
Confederates. By rapid stages, the "Vindictives"
raised the bewildered negro to the dignity of the
franchise and gave into his hands control of state
and local government in the South. To make the
humiliation of Southerners more painful, these
"Black Republican" governments were supported
by white men of questionable character and motive who gathered from both North and South.
It was this ordeal that created the "Solid South."

The war did not solve the negro problem; it only modified conditions. That question still remains.

Throughout the struggle between the American states, Europe had looked on with strangely mixed emotions. British manufacturers were dependent upon Southern cotton. The British nobility was sympathetic with the aristocratic cotton-planter and indifferent to the lot of the negro slave. But the middle classes and notably the laborers in the English cotton-mills were devoted to the North because of anti-slavery feeling. It needed only Lincoln's Emancipation Proclamation and the prospect of Federal victory to turn British opinion to the Northern side. Southern agents saw vanish the hope that Great Britain would recognize Southern independence. Southern bonds lost all attractiveness for British capital. After the war Great Britain accepted the decision of the Geneva Tribunal. Damages were awarded to the United States for depredations by the Confederate commerce-raiders which had been fitted out in British ports.

France under Napoleon III gave secret aid to Southern agents, talked openly of interference if Great Britain would co-operate, and dreamed of another French empire in America. French troops

appeared in North America and set Maximilian of Austria upon a Mexican throne. But the enthusiasm of Napoleon III was rapidly destroyed by the coolness of Great Britain. The troops in Mexico retired before the menaces of the triumphant North, leaving Maximilian to his fate.

The Burst of War Volume 29, Chapter VI
  The impossible situation at Fort Sumter
    The question of relief for Anderson
    Demands of the South
      The first shot Volume 30, Pages 14–23
      The fall of Sumter Volume 31, Pages 1–16
  Lumbering machines of war " " Pages 16–55
    Washington in peril
      Citizen armies at Bull Run
        The flight to Washington
    Competition for the border states Volume 29, Pages 145–147
      Blair and Lyon in Missouri
      Anderson in Kentucky
      McClellan in West Virginia
  The antagonists Volume 31, Chapter II
    The advantages of the South
    The potential superiority of the North
      The advantage of sea power
    Conscription

Military and Naval Operations
  The naval war of 1862 Volume 31, Chapter III
    The blockade
    The *Monitor* and the *Merrimac*
    Farragut at New Orleans
      A futile expedition up the Mississippi
  The river war of 1862 Volume 31, Chapter IV
    Operations down the Mississippi
      Halleck versus A. S. Johnston
        Grant, commander in the field

Military and Naval Operations—Continued

 Forts Henry and Donelson
  Keys to the Cumberland and Tennessee river valleys
  Grant's victory
 Pope's capture of Island No. Ten
 Johnston's drive against Grant at Shiloh
  Pittsburg Landing on the Tennessee River
  The errors of Grant
  The Confederate failure
 A northern caterpillar
  Halleck's approach upon Corinth
 The advance of the northern river fleet down the Mississippi
  The capture of Memphis
 Confederate counter advances
  A triple offensive   Compare Volume 30, Page 44
   Bragg into Kentucky
   Price and Van Dorn against Grant at Memphis and Corinth
   Lee into Maryland
 Grant's attempts to reach down the Mississippi to Vicksburg
 The futile "War in the West"
  The campaign in New Mexico
 Battles and maneuvers in Virginia, 1862–1863
         Volume 31, Chapter VI

 McClellan's peninsular campaign
  The McDowell corps
 The genius of Stonewall Jackson
  A brilliant campaign in the Shenandoah Valley
   The effect upon McClellan
 Southern strategy against McClellan
  The confederate attack at Fair Oaks
  Stuart's ride around McClellan
  The arrival of Jackson from the Shenandoah
  The Seven Days' Battles, June 26, 1862
   Richmond made secure
  Pope's army of Virginia

Military and Naval Operations—Continued

    The strategy of Lee and Jackson

      Second Bull Run, August 29, 1862

    Lee's first invasion: part of a triple offensive

      Maryland unresponsive

      The return of McClellan to command

        Antietam, September 17, 1862

         Its diplomatic value to the North

                      Volume 31, Page 178

        Stuart's second ride around McClellan

    Burnside's attempt to cope with Lee and Jackson

      The battle of Fredericksburg, December 13, 1862

        The North appalled

    Another northern commander

    "Fighting Joe Hooker"

    The handicaps of Lee

      The confederate plan of battle

      Chancellorsville, May 1–3, 1863

        The death of Jackson

    Lee's second invasion   Volume 31, Chapter VIII

      Pennsylvania, Northern storehouse

      Hooker replaced by Meade

      The battle of Gettysburg, July 3, 1863

        Pickett's charge

        Lee's retreat

The triumph of Grant, 1863   Volume 31, Chapter VII

  The fall of Vicksburg

    The co-operation of Porter's fleet

    Grant's campaign below Vicksburg

      His march on Jackson

      The investment of Vicksburg

        Re-established lines to the North

        The siege

        Pemberton's surrender

  The Confederates in Tennessee

    Morgan's raid across the Ohio

    The retirement of Bragg

      The Federal occupation of Chattanooga

Military and Naval Operations—Continued
>   The Confederate turn at Chickamauga, September
>   19, 1863
>   The failure of Rosecrans
>   The stand of Thomas
>   The investment of Chattanooga
>   Grant on the defense
>   The change to attack, November 24, 1863
>   Missionary Ridge
>   Lookout Mountain
>   Hooker's fame
> The naval war, 1863–1864   Volume 31, Chapter IX
>   Blockade runners
>   The tightening grip of the North
>   The career of the *Alabama*
>   Southern raider
>   Defeat by the U. S. S. *Kearsarge*, June 19, 1864, off
>   Cherbourg, France
>   Farragut in Mobile Bay, August 5, 1864
>   The Confederate ram, *Albemarle*
>   Roanoke River, the outlet of North Carolina
>   The exploit of Lieutenant W. B. Cushing, U. S. N.,
>   October 27, 1864
>   The fall of Fort Fisher, January 15, 1865
>   The defenses of Wilmington, North Carolina
>   The best southern port
> The grand attack on the Confederacy, 1864
>   Volume 31, Chapter X
>
>   Grant's plan: Converging thrusts
>   His drive against Lee
>   Richmond, the objective
>   Sherman against Johnston
>   Atlanta, the objective
>   Farragut and Banks
>   Mobile, the objective
>   The meddling of Stanton
>   The fiasco of the Red River expedition
>   The race for Richmond
>   Grant in the Wilderness

Military and Naval Operations—Continued
        Sheridan's raid behind Lee
        The horror of Cold Harbor
        The change of plans
        The siege of Richmond
        Early's dash on Washington
        Sheridan in the Shenandoah
        Sherman's approach to Atlanta   Volume 31, Chapter XI
        The Fabian retreat of Johnston
        The interference of Davis
        Sherman's victory over Hood
        The fall of Atlanta
        Sherman's march through Georgia to the sea
        Destruction of the Confederate storehouse
        Hood's sortie into Tennessee
        His defeat before Nashville by Thomas
   The end of military resistance, 1865   Volume 31, Chapter XII
        The death grip
        Grant encircling Richmond
        Sherman marching north through the Carolinas
        Lee's flight
        The surrender at Appomattox, April 9, 1865

Europe and the War   Volume 29, Chapter VII
  Rivalry for the support of Great Britain
                  Volume 30, Chapter III
    Munitions
    The sale of Federal and Confederate bonds
  The sting of the Northern blockade
    British pride
      The Trent affair
    The market for Southern cotton
      The sufferings of British textile workers
  The temptations of "recognition"
    British uncertainties
      The issue of slavery
        The effect of the Emancipation Proclamation
  The ambition of France   Volume 30, Chapter VIII
    Confederate spell-binders

Europe and the War—Continued
    Napoleonic promises
        Their collapse

The Greatest Figure   Volume 29, Chapters VII, VIII
    Lincoln's statecraft
        The Union foremost   Volume 31, Chapter V
        The border states
    A coalition cabinet
        War Democrats
    Emancipation
        An instrument of war
        A diplomatic weapon
    The use of power
        Conscription
        The suspension of *Habeas Corpus*
    Manager of men
        His subordinates: Seward, Chase, and Stanton
        His generals
            Fremont and McClellan
            His letter to Hooker   Volume 31, Page 289
            Grant
        Advisers
            Busybody Congressmen
            Horace Greeley
    The peace party
        Copperheads
        Vallandigham
    The humanitarian
        Deserters
        Sorrowing mothers
        The defeated South

The Home Front in the North
    Finance   Volume 29, Chapter X
        Chase, Secretary of the Treasury
            Quarrels with Seward
        His political aspirations
            Candidacy in 1864
               The Pomeroy circular

The Home Front in the North—Continued
    The question of taxes or loans
    The suspension of specie payments
      Issues of treasury notes
      "Greenbacks"
        Irredeemable paper
        Chase compromised
    The service of Jay Cooke
      Sales of bonds
        The turning point in war finance
    The National Bank Act of 1863
  The effects of the war on domestic life
    The loss of the nation's best
    The opportunity for the profiteer
      Speculators in blood
    A remarkable increase in Northern business
      The shift of labor
        Westward migration
          The Homestead Act, 1862
          Little pauperism
        Immigration
        The labor of women
          Labor-saving machines on the farms
    The freedom of the "disloyals"
      Army supplies
        The protest of the Boston Board of Trade
        The woolen manufactures
          Vaulting dividends
          "Shoddy millionaires"
  The defeatist movement   Volume 29, Chapter XIII
    The culmination in 1864
      The Cleveland Convention
        Fremont
        Wendell Phillips, Abolitionist
      The Knights of the Golden Circle
        Underground politicians
        Malcontents
        Draft-dodgers
        Confederate agents

The Home Front in the North—Continued
    The Sons of Liberty
      Lesser secret societies
    The sinister figure of Vallandigham
                            Volume 29, Pages 162–167
      Morgan's raid
    The Chicago plot, June, 1864
      The assembly of the Democratic national convention
      The failure of the plot
        The cowardice of the Sons of Liberty
    The Democratic nomination
      McClellan
        The presence of Seymour and Belmont of New York
        Vallandigham's resolutions
        McClellan's rejection of the platform
    The renomination of Lincoln
      Johnson, War Democrat, for Vice-President
      Factional quarrels
        Lincoln's dispute with Congress over reconstruction
        The Wade-Davis Manifesto
          The Vindictives
        Horace Greeley
          His negotiations with Confederates in Canada
             Failure
          His adherence to the vindictive group
        Blair and Chase
          Lincoln's adroit management of their resignations
      News from Mobile and Atlanta
        The victories of Farragut and Sherman
    The re-election of Lincoln
      The determination of the people

The Home Front in the South
    Davis, a misfit   Volume 30, Chapter II
      Immediate antagonisms
        Rhett and Yancey

The Home Front in the South—Continued
>>>> Ignored secessionists
>>> The necessity for Southern nationality
>>> The impossibility of States Rights
>>>> The contrast of South Carolina and Mississippi
>>> The clash of state and Confederate authority
>>>> Central control of the army
>>>> Conscription
>>>> The suspension of *Habeas Corpus*
>>>> Martial law in the cities
>> The reaction against Davis   Volume 30, Chapter IV
>>> The wave of alarm
>>>> The surrender of Fort Donelson
>>> Secret sessions of the government
>>>> Yancey's protest
>>> The hostility of Rhett's *Charleston Mercury* and Pollard's *Richmond Examiner*
>>> The factious governor of Georgia
>>> The sinister figure of Benjamin
>>>> Attorney General
>>>> Secretary of War
>>>> Secretary of State
>>> Davis' mismanagement of his generals
>>>> Bragg, Johnston, Lee
>>> The tangle of prices and supplies
>>>> Regulation
>>>> Taxes in kind
>>> The outcry against the suspension of *Habeas Corpus*
> The disintegration of the Confederacy
>> The crisis of 1863   Volume 30, Chapter V
>>> Angry attacks on Davis
>>>> The conduct of the war
>>>> The impressment of supplies
>>>>> The bitterness of middle-class farmers
>>>>>> North Carolina
>>>> Davis' obsession with his military prowess
>> The torture of war   Volume 30, Chapter VI
>>> The effect upon the cherished institution of slavery
>>> The hardships of the people

The Home Front in the South—Continued
   Planter and poor man alike
   The ordeals of women
  The blockade
   Scarcity of medicines and clothing
  The collapse of the railroad system
  The curse of war
   Speculators in food
 The turn of fortune   Volume 30, Chapter VII
  The loss of the Mississippi River
  The failure of Lee in Pennsylvania
  The defeat at Chattanooga
  The last stand
   The defense of the Old South
    The heart of the Confederacy
   The remonstrance of outlying sections
    The head of treason raised
     "Heroes of America"
   Negotiations in Canada
    The cowardice of the northern defeatists
  Failure in Europe   Volume 30, Chapter VIII
 Desperate remedies   " "   IX
  Brown's efforts to save Georgia
   Sneers for Davis
  The "people's war" against Sherman
  The despair of South Carolina
   Helplessness in the hands of Sherman
  Schemes for new associations of the states
   The abandonment of Virginia
  Lee for military dictator
   A myth
   Lee made commander-in-chief
  The frantic efforts of the Confederate Treasury
  The rage against Davis
   The congressional attack
    The elevation of Lee
 The peace movement   Volume 30, Chapter X
  Bands of Unionists
  The peasant farmers of North Carolina

The Home Front in the South—Continued
>> The role of Stephens
>>> An ante-bellum Whig
>>>> The conference with Lincoln at Hampton Roads
>> The last stake of the South   Volume 30, Chapter XI
>>> The arming of slaves
>>>> Emancipation as a reward
>>>>> The refusal of the planters
>>>>> Lee's support
>>>>>> Rejection by Virginia
>>> The failure of the plan
>> The flight of Davis   "   "   XII
>>> Blind resolution

Reconstruction
> The affliction of the South   Volume 32, Chapter I
>> Society disorganized
>>> Displaced Confederates and Unionists
>> The land devastated
>>> A shortage of materials and men
>>> Slave property wiped out
>> Lines of communication broken down
>> Confiscations by the Federal government
>>> Distressing frauds
> The attitude of the North
>> Measures of relief
>> The annoyance of Federal garrisons
>>> Negro troops
>> The appearance of the carpetbagger
>> Conflicting reports to the northern public
>>> The creation of misunderstandings
>>>> The contrast of Grant and Schurz
>>> The statements of southern leaders, Hampton and Lee
> The bewilderment of the negro   Volume 32, Chapter II
>> His ideas of freedom
>> Morals and manners
>> Negro suffrage

Reconstruction—Continued

The mercy of Lincoln   Volume 32, Chapter III
 His way of restoring peace in the South
          Volume 29, Chapter XIV
 The re-establishment of state governments by the people themselves
 Johnson's clumsy execution
  The resentment of the Vindictives
   Sumner and Stevens
   The descent to brawling personalities
The perplexing status of the negro Volume 32, Chapter IV
 Neither slaves nor citizens
 The Southern solution
  Black laws
   Inferiority to the whites
    Racial separation
   Special treatment
    Vagrancy
    Apprenticeship
    Marriage
 Northern assistance
  The Freedman's Bureau
   Aid and advice
   Medical supplies and sales of land
   The wages of the negroes
  Mismanagement and abuse
   Meddling in politics
The triumph of the Vindictives Volume 32, Chapter V
 The Congressional plan of reconstruction
  The Wade-Davis Bill
   The veto by Lincoln
  Failure to control Johnson
 The political question
  Confederate Congressmen or negro voters
   The dominance of the Republican Party threatened
 The contest with Johnson
  The extension of the Freedman's Bureau
  The Civil Rights Act
  The Fourteenth Amendment

Reconstruction—Continued

        Johnson's advice to the states to reject

      Congressional elections, 1866

        Johnson's "Swing around the Circle"

        The Fourteenth Amendment rejected by the South

        The defeat of Johnson's candidates

      Actions of Congress in 1867

        Insults to Johnson

          The Tenure of Office Act

          The army appropriation rider

          The Reconstruction Acts of March

      Stanton and Johnson   Volume 32, Chapter VII

        The impeachment of the President

        Political jobbery

Military rule in the South   Volume 32, Chapter VI

    The major-generals

      Authority from Congress

      Their conservatism

    The opportunity for Republican growth in the South

      Registration of the negro

      Protection for his vote

    The state conventions

      Carpetbaggers, scalawags, and negroes

        Constitution-makers

      Readmission to the Union by Congress

        Recognition of the radical governments

    The retirement of the generals

Informal war

    Northern forces of perversion   Volume 32, Chapter VIII

      The Union League

        Control of the negro

          The delusion of secret ritual

        Military discipline

          The elimination of black Democrats

    Radical state governments   Volume 32, Chapter X

      Disfranchisement of the Confederates

      The power of the carpetbagger

        The organizer of negro rule

      Burlesque government

Reconstruction—Continued

    Southern resistance   Volume 32, Chapter **XI**

      The Ku Klux Klan

        The organization of the white population

        The intimidation of the negro

          His disappearance from the polls

  Disheartening effects of reconstruction

    The gulf between the churches of the North and South

                                 Volume 32, Chapter **IX**

    The formation of negro churches

    The blight upon education

      Radical control of the universities

      The effect of mixed schools

    The changing South   "   "   **XII**

      Industrial hardships

      The desperation of the planter

        Vanishing labor

          The shiftless freedman

      The pernicious credit system

    The "Solid South"

      Iron in the soul of the white man

The failure of reconstruction   "   "   **XIII**

    The success of Southern resistance

    The development of tolerance in the North

    The diversion of corruption in Northern governments

      The rise of new sectional controversies

      The effect of foreign issues

      The reaction against negro suffrage in Northern states

    The Liberal Republican movement

      Grant's change of policy

        The Amnesty Act, 1872

      The crisis of 1876: "the bloody shirt"

        The tacit understanding with President Hayes

    New ways in the South

      The abandonment of the Ku Klux method

      The control of ballot boxes

      Literacy tests

      Residence requirements

        The elimination of the negro vote

The French Menace in Mexico   Volume 29, Chapter XII

The dreams of Napoleon III
> The United States torn by civil war
>> The Monroe Doctrine dormant
> The occupation of Mexico
>> Intrigues with the Confederate States

         Volume 30, Chapter VIII
         "   "   Pages 178–179

The policy forced upon Lincoln and Seward
> Adroit hints to Napoleon
> Congressional vehemence
>> Presidential evasion
>>> The assistance of Sumner in the Senate
> The failure of the Confederacy
> An end to Napoleon's enterprise

Napoleon bowed out of Mexico by Seward

         Volume 46, Pages 56–58

The arbitration of claims against Great Britain
         Volume 46, Pages 31–38

Irritation in the Civil War
> Great Britain's recognition of the South as belligerent
> The Trent affair
>> The acknowledged mistake of the North
> Confederate rams and commerce-raiders
>> Products of British shipyards
> The *Alabama* and the *Florida*
>> The destruction of Northern commerce
> The Fenian raid into Canada from the North

The American claims against Great Britain
> Property destroyed
> Indirect losses
>> Insurance
>> The cost of pursuit
>> The prolongation of the war
>>> The fury of Sumner
>> British refusal to negotiate

President Grant
> The repudiation of Sumner's demands

CHAPTER XVI

THE RISE OF BIG BUSINESS

DURING the first sixty years of the Nineteenth Century the United States grew until it nearly equalled in area the whole of Europe, the most amazing feat of expansion and settlement that the world had ever known. The American people were still moving rapidly and steadily westward to fill up the empty spaces when a grim war between the states all but split the nation into two. Few Americans realized, when this struggle was ended, that their country was on the verge of an industrial expansion as amazing as the territorial growth which had preceded. By the middle of the century many European nations had advanced far into a new industrial civilization. The United States still remained largely a nation of pioneering farmers. Hidden in the territory of the young nation was mineral wealth surpassing all European conceptions. Yet at the end of the Civil

War, he would have been a bold American indeed who would have predicted that, before the century had ended, his country would have outstripped the world's greatest industrial nations in organization and production.

In 1865, business was conducted on what seems by subsequent standards a small scale. There were some corporations, notably to build railroads, but most of the nation's commerce and industry was in the hands of private individuals. Familiar evidences of the new order were lacking: "the cities of skyscrapers, the long miles of steel rails and telegraph poles, the gigantic railroad terminals, the great bridges across the rivers, the many-windowed factories with their tall chimneys, their clouds of smoke and their flaming furnaces." The business man of the Sixties did not have the money, the labor, the ability to accumulate materials, nor the organization to produce these results; but, in the span of a generation they were accomplished. During the first quarter of the Twentieth Century, America forged rapidly ahead into a position of unquestioned economic superiority over the rest of the world.

Five things brought it about: communications improved for the transportation of materials and

the transmission of ideas over vast distances; new machines of tremendous power and wonderful dexterity; labor to direct the machines and do the work which only men could do; organization to co-ordinate the multitude of operations and to regulate the activities of the laborers employed in the process of manufacture and sale; and concentration of capital to furnish the financial power necessary for the formation of gigantic enterprises. Underneath all was the basic factor of America's wealth in natural resources.

Strong leaders appeared to build up those great enterprises. They warred among themselves, with a ruthlessness in their early conflicts reminiscent of the battles by which the red man had been driven from his hunting grounds. The strongest and most fortunate won. Then they began to unite for the purpose of forming still greater enterprises. The corporation became the "trust"; competition broke down. Much of the wealth created by the new developments passed into the control of a powerful few. They became industrial giants who gathered into their own hands the factories and systems of transportation of the nation. America, and then the world, became their market. Again and again they sur-

passed their competitors abroad. They accumulated wealth hitherto undreamed of. When the Great War shook Europe to its foundations, their financial center became the financial center of the world, and the economic power which they had amassed became a powerful factor in checking rampant militarism.

They were few, these industrial giants, yet they were but the leaders of an army of business men out of whose ranks they had come and whence new figures were constantly emerging. Thus, the old American ideal of democracy passed over into the new era. The pioneer spirit of the old frontier stirred the farsighted organizer in the new order. The qualities of courage, aggressiveness, and steadfastness that had marked the rough origins of America marked also the strenuous development of the newer civilization. As the Nineteenth Century passed, the task of creating a nation in a wilderness had nearly reached completion.

The Evolution of Big Business   Volume 39, Chapter I
   The contrast of yesterday and today
    The new vocabulary of business
    The advent of large-scale production
      The growth of corporations
    The substitution of combination for competition
    The appearance of great fortunes
      Merchant princes replaced by captains of industry

The Evolution of Big Business—Continued
    The effects of the Civil War
        Stimulation of production in the North
        The rapid increase of immigration
        Changes in the routes of transportation
        The birth of industries
            Woolen mills
            Shoe factories
        The migration of the unemployed across the Mississippi
        Commodore Vanderbilt, pioneer of the new age

Railroad Building
    The expansion of Eastern railroads   Volume 38, Pages 13–19
        The New York Central   "   "   Pages 29–46
            Cornelius Vanderbilt
                The construction of a system
                Feeding lines
        The Pennsylvania   "   "   Pages 50–63
            A state system
            Connections with the West and the East
                The tunnel into New York City
            Non-speculative management
            "Community of interest"
                Other railroads
        The Erie   Volume 38, Pages 71–94
            "The football of Wall Street"
            Drew, expert at fleecing
            His war with Vanderbilt
                The corruption of legislatures
                    Jay Gould at Albany
            Systematic looting
            Stabilization by Morgan interests
                A coal carrier
        The Baltimore and Ohio   Volume 38, Pages 102–120
            Prosperity with Garrett!
                Dividends paid from capital
                Disillusionment
            Competition with the Pennsylvania

Railroad Building—Continued
    Evil days
    The restoration by Morgan interests
    "Community of interest"
    The Pennsylvania
    Harriman
      The Union Pacific
    Willard, the modern railroad executive
Rails from coast to coast
  Construction of the Union Pacific
    Competition with the Central Pacific
    Land grants
    Building scandals
      The Credit Mobilier   Compare Volume 43, Page 43
  Rival routes into the Central West
  Consolidations and railroad wars
    The figures of Harriman and Huntington
      The expansion of the Union Pacific
      The Southern Pacific
      The Oregon roads
Development of the Pacific Northwest
                Volume 38, Chapter VII
  The Northern Pacific
  The enterprise of Jay Cooke
    The Panic of 1873
    Receivership
  Villard and German capital
    The crash of 1893
  The entrance of Morgan
    The alliance with Hill
  The spectacular contest between Hill and Harriman
                Volume 41, Chapter VI
    Their understanding   Volume 47, Pages 91–93
      The Northern Securities Company
        Dissolution by the decision of the Supreme
        Court
Hill's Great Northern   Volume 38, Chapter IX
  Beginnings with the St. Paul and Pacific
  Trade on the Red River with Winnipeg

Railroad Building—Continued
    The future Lord Strathcona
    The wheat crop of 1877
    Hill's dream of a road to the Pacific
    Successful business methods
        Low operating costs
    Control of the Burlington
  Development of the new Southwest Volume 38, Chapter VIII
    The Santa Fé
        Penetration into New Mexico
        Competition with the Southern Pacific
           Connections with the East at Chicago
        Progress under Ripley
  Railroads in the South   Volume 38, Chapter X
    The Southern Railway system
        The temporary interest of the Pennsylvania
    Brice and organization
    The hard times of 1893
        The services of Morgan
  Harriman, railroad romancer   Volume 38, Chapter XI
    The Illinois Central
    The Union Pacific
        Support by Kuhn, Loeb and Company
           The absorption of the Oregon lines
           The struggle with Huntington's Southern Pacific
    The clash with Hill   Volume 41, Chapter VI
        The contest for the Burlington   Volume 47, Page 91
        The scramble for Northern Pacific shares
           Compromise and merger
              The Northern Securities Company
                Dissolution by the Supreme Court
  Visions in the East
    Harriman's negotiations for the New York Central
    Domination over the Baltimore and Ohio
        A coast to coast system
        Lines north and south
  Present policies
    Abandonment of expansion
    Efficient operation

Railroad Building—Continued
          Changing public sentiment
               More stringent regulation of railroads
     The railroad problem today   Volume 38, Chapter XII
          The effects of speculation and stock-jobbing
          The attitude of the farmer
                              Compare Volume 45, Chapters III–IV
                                   and Volume 45, Page 129–143, 198
          Demands for government legislation
               Granger laws
               Railroad rate laws
                    Public servants or private enterprises?
                    The struggle in Illinois
                         Maximum fares
                         Freight charges based upon distance
                         The state railroad commission
                              Munn versus Illinois
                              The public interest upheld
          Partial success of the railroads
               Manipulation of service
               The problem of interstate traffic
                    The way cleared for the Federal Interstate
                         Commerce Commission
                         The Wabash case   Volume 38, Page 232
          The transition from expansion to efficient operation
               Demands for lower rates
          The decline of the theory of competition
               The necessity for monopoly
               The growth of the conception, public service cor-
                    porations
          The increasing power of the Interstate Commerce
               Commission
               Roosevelt's administration   Volume 38, Pages 233–235
                                   Compare Volume 47, Chapter VII
     A new principle
          The power of Congress to fix railroad wages
               The Adamson law   Compare Volume 40, Chapter VII
                    Threats of the brotherhoods
                    The decision of the Supreme Court

Railroad Building—Continued
    The railroads in the World War
        Governmental control
           Operation as a single system
                      Volume 37, Pages 146–156

Great Inventions
  Agents of communication
    Presses, linotypes, typewriters
    Phonographs and cameras
      Edison and Eastman
      Motion pictures
  Electricity, servant of man   " "   Chapter IX
    Pioneers
      Gilbert, Franklin, and Henry
    Achievements after the Civil War
      The arc light
        Brush
      The work of Edison
        Multiplex telegraphy
        Incandescent lamps
        Motors and batteries
      Westinghouse and others
      The telephone
        Bell and Gray   Compare Volume 39, Pages 86–100
  The airplane   Volume 37, Chapter X
    Franklin and the balloon
    Langley's experiments
    The Wrights
    Glenn Curtis and the seaplane
      The flight of the NC4
    Commercial air routes

Industrial Giants
  The first trust   Volume 39, Chapter II
    Creation of the Standard Oil Company
      The discovery of petroleum in Pennsylvania
        Kier and Bissell
        Drake's folly
        Van Syckel's pipe line

Industrial Giants—Continued

    The career of John D. Rockefeller
      Refineries
      His assets
        Adequate capital
        Technical resources
      Absorption of rival companies
        The purchasing campaign
      A marketing system
    The South Improvement Company
      The railroad rebate
        The responsibility of the Pennsylvania Railroad
        The part of Rockefeller
      The soul of the New York Central
      Violation of the law
    Ruthless war on competing refineries
      Cut-throat sales
      The bribery of railroad agents
      "Bogus companies"
    The Trust
      The suit of Ohio
        Organization in New Jersey
      The decision of the United States Supreme Court
        Nominal dissolution   Compare Volume 47, Page 93
    Reappearance of competition
      New discoveries of petroleum
      Rival companies
  Steel
    Kelly and the Bessemer process
    Iron ore about Lake Superior
    The union of Superior ore and Pennsylvania coal
      The genius of Carnegie   Compare Volume 41,
                                        Chapter III

        His ability to pick men
          Their pace-maker
      Phipps, Frick, and Schwab
        The accountant
        The coke-maker
        The handler of men

Industrial Giants—Continued

    The share of the railroad and ore-boat

    Other steel kingdoms

      Birmingham in Alabama

      Colorado

        Rockefeller interests

    John W. Gates, gambler

      Texas cattle and barbed wire

        The American Steel & Wire Company

    The battle of giants   Compare Volume 41, Chapter V

      The desire of Carnegie to sell out

        His antipathy for Wall Street

        His elusive price

          The encroachment of Wall Street into steel
            manufacturing

          Carnegie's counter-trusts

      The nervousness of Wall Street

        The capitulation of Morgan to Carnegie

      The organization of the United States Steel
      Corporation

The Telephone   Volume 39, Chapter IV

  Bell's invention

    His many successors in improvement

  Vail's business genius

    The vision of national service

  The war between the Bell company and the Western
    Union Telegraph

  The treaty of peace

    Consolidation

      The Western Electric

        Factory for telephone apparatus

  The American Telephone and Telegraph Company

    A national public-service corporation

Public Utilities   Volume 39, Chapter V

  Street car lines in the United States

  Gas and electric light companies

    The scramble for franchise

      A sordid phase of American life

        Municipal politics

Industrial Giants—Continued
       "Graft"
      Speculation
       "Wall Street"
    Yerkes's hold on Chicago
    Widener and Philadelphia
      His rise from butcher to boss
    The strange career of W. C. Whitney in New York
      The noiseless co-operation of Thomas Fortune
         Ryan
  The great syndicate
    "The holding company"
      Profitable leases
      Construction accounts
    "Prying eyes" thwarted
      The public
    The escape of the "inside gentlemen"
      The Metropolitan unloaded on investors
      Its crash in 1907   Compare Volume 41, Chapter VIII
                         Volume 47, Page 101
  Public protection
  State utility commissions
Farm machinery   Volume 39, Chapter VI
  McCormick and the reaper
    The amazement of Europe
  Succeeding improvements
    The harvester
    The twine-binder
  Development of large scale production
    Sales efficiency
  The International Harvester Company
    Combination instead of competition
    The work of Perkins
The automobile   Volume 39, Chapter VII
  An uncertain infancy
  A youth of giant stature
  Henry Ford's conception
    A car for every family
  The tools of American industry

Industrial Giants—Continued
    Quantity production
    Standardization
    Labor-saving machinery
  The contrast of Vanderbilt and Ford
  The change of industrial ideals

The Rôle of the Financier
  The greatest power in finance   Volume 41, Chapter I
    The origin of the Morgan interests
      George Peabody in London
        Partnership with Junius Morgan
      John Pierpont Morgan
        Alliance with Dabney
        The Drexels
      Competition with Jay Cooke
        Finance in the Civil War
      Success with the French loan
  Morgan, railroad financier Compare Volume 38, Chapter II
    The Long Island Railroad
    The rescue of Vanderbilt
      The New York Central
      The discomfiture of Jay Gould
    The chaos of the eighties
      The union of the West Shore with the New York
        Central
      Reorganization of the Philadelphia and Reading
      Aid for the Baltimore and Ohio
      The Chesapeake and Ohio
    The Southern Railway system
      Morgan's protection of English investors
    Drastic remedies for the Erie
      Morgan's "voting trust"
    Steadying hands for other roads
      The Hocking Valley
      The Northern Pacific
      The Santa Fé
      The Lehigh Valley
      The Central of Georgia

The Rôle of the Financier—Continued

Workers in iron	Volume 41, Chapter III
Carnegie, accumulator of wealth	
Steel transformed into gold	
Frick's coke	
Rockefeller's ore fields	
The intrusion of high finance	" " Chapter V
The vogue of consolidation	Volume 39, Chapter III
The resistance of Carnegie	
The offer of Moore	
The advances of Rockefeller	
Morgan's contest with Carnegie	
Rival plants	
The capitulation of Morgan	
Schwab as intermediary	
The price of a Scotchman	
The Steel Trust	
Threat, finesse, and purchase	
Morgan, Perkins, and Gary	
Rockefeller won by Frick	
The Standard Oil in finance	Volume 41, Chapter IV
	Compare Volume 39, Chapter II
Early independence of banking interests	
Cash reserves	
A bank within an industry	
Participation in the affairs of Wall Street	
The absorption of the City Bank	
The work of Stillman	
The Chicago, Milwaukee & St. Paul Railroad	
Support for Harriman and the Union Pacific	
Promotion of the Amalgamated Copper Company	
Interest in public utilities	
Alliance with W. C. Whitney	
The "Money Power"	
Morgan overshadowed	
High Finance	Volume 41, Chapter VI
The sport of duelling with railroads	
Harriman and Fish	
The Illinois Central	

The Rôle of the Financier—Continued
>Harriman and Schiff
>>The Union Pacific
>Harriman and Hill   Compare Volume 38, Chapter VII
>>>>>>>>>>>>>>Volume 47, Pages 91–93

>>The Burlington
>>The Northern Pacific
>>>Rockefeller versus Morgan
>>The compromise
>>>The Northern Securities Company
>Professional manipulators of railroads
>>Gates and Hawley
>>>The Louisville & Nashville
>>The Moores and Reid
>>>The Rock Island
>The culmination of consolidation
>>>>>>>>>Volume 41, Chapter VII
>>The International Mercantile Marine
>>>Transatlantic shipping
>>The International Harvester Company
>>The General Electric Company
>>The close linking of railroad systems
>>The alliances of life insurance companies with trust
>>>companies
>>>Public investigation, 1905
>>>>The fame of Hughes
>>>Congressional investigation, 1913   Volume 41, Appx.
>>>>The processes of concentration
>>>>Agents
>>>>The peril of the nation
>The turn of 1907   Volume 41, Chapter VIII
>>Schwab and Bethlehem steel
>>Morse and coastwise shipping
>>The panic
>>>The result of "high finance"
>>>The failure of Morse
>>>The crash of the Knickerbocker Trust Company
>>>Morgan's rescue of the Tennessee Company
>>>>Violation of the Sherman Anti-Trust Law

CHAPTER XVII

THE CONSEQUENCES OF INDUSTRIALISM

AMERICAN life had to adjust itself to the new industrial order which came after the Civil War. The American conception of democracy, an equal chance for everyone, gave opportunity for a few strong men to climb to dizzy heights of fortune and power, but laboring men stumbled over one another and got nowhere. Farmers found themselves in a new situation. Before the War they had formed so large a part of the population that they had never thought of themselves as a separate group. In the forty years after 1860 the population of the nation more than doubled. Of that great increase the larger part massed in the cities, making them huge congested areas presenting strange problems to the new generation. By 1920, city dwellers outnumbered the rural population. Economists estimate that now every husbandman must produce food enough for three

families. Both laboring man and farmer rapidly became conscious of their special interests. Each group turned to collective action to protect itself in the contest with the rising power of capitalism.

Laborers endeavored to obtain better wages and working conditions but they were not able to keep pace with the growing strength of the employer. As a result, times that were particularly hard drove the wage-earner to violence. The terrors of 1877, 1886, and 1894 impressed upon thinking men that all was not well in American society even if huge corporations were towering above ordinary business structures and some men grew fabulously rich. During the Eighties it seemed as though the secret organization, the Knights of Labor, might draw the laboring class into one big union. But its radical excesses in 1886 discredited the organization. It collapsed with unexpected suddenness. The American Federation of Labor, based on sounder principles, took its place as the national body of organized labor. Apart from the Federation have grown up four strong railroad brotherhoods. Together, they have held in check radical elements within their organizations, scorning the "Reds" as un-American. But they have failed to put labor in the place of power that it desires

and that in some industrial countries it has attained.

The ranks of American labor have been swelled by a host of Europeans who came to man machines in the new factories, to lay railroad tracks, and to mine coal and metals for America's industries. The appeal of high wages and cheap land in America was felt throughout Europe. Prior to the Civil War the north of Europe had furnished the majority of those who sought the United States, but, as American industry grew, the main source shifted to Mediterranean countries. A few of these newcomers struck out as of old for the frontier but most of them crowded into the great manufacturing cities. Their babble of foreign tongues and confusion of national prejudices defied the process of Americanization that had worked rapidly among the earlier immigrants. The test of the World War brought sharply into view the failures of the American "melting pot." The conviction has grown upon the American people that the flood of aliens must be checked if the racial character of the nation is to be preserved. The old policy of welcome to all has been replaced by close restriction.

No more marked was the effect of industrialism

on labor than on the farmer. As Eastern capitalists spread a web of railroads over the continent, the Western homesteaders became conscious of common interests with the farmers of the Ohio and Mississippi river valleys and of the South. Railroad monopolies and high freight rates goaded the farmers to take collective action in Granges and Alliances. Many state legislatures passed "Grange Laws" to regulate the railroads. In the long run, however, the agrarian organizations failed. Most spectacular of all was the defeat of the Populist party in 1896. In the Twentieth Century the farmers have learned the art of organization and now enjoy the political power which it brings.

The new industrial age has made significant changes in the South. When the ordeal of Reconstruction had passed, the Southerners faced the task of building a new civilization upon the ruins of the old. The negro was a freeman. The white man staggered under a load of public and private debt. Yet, in less than half a century a new South has emerged. Its life, although different from that of the rest of the nation, shows unmistakably that forces operating in the West and North are also active in the Cotton Kingdom. The small

farmer has usurped the place once held by the old
aristocratic planter and, like the western farmer,
has caught the meaning of organization. As industrialism has worked its way southward, mines,
steel mills, and textile factories have increased.
A new white labor group has formed. But the
negro question, from earliest times the peculiar
problem of the South, remains — as yet un-
answered.

Industrialism created a New South. It brought
new problems to the laborer and the farmer. The
whole economic foundation of the nation was
changing and in adjustment to it the entire super-
structure of American civilization was being re-
built. If the factories created great cities, hu-
manitarianism sought to relieve the misery and
degradation of the slum. Religion offered the
mission, the Salvation Army, and the Christian
Associations. Rich churches that had supported
the struggling missionaries on the frontier now
also established outposts among the poor. Education took on a new significance as the public
school became the center of Americanization. As
the tasks of the new day had become intricate,
colleges and universities turned to the training of
specialists. There was little time for quiet medi-

tation. Men of letters appeared here and there, but their message was not matured, for they lived in a time of transition. They were linked to the men of the Fifties who had brought American literature into flower and pointed the way to the future when the ideals and emotions of the new order should become articulate.

The Story of Labor
  Industrial anarchy after the Civil War Volume 40, Chapter IV
    Panics close upon prosperity
      The anguish of labor
    Strikes
      The terrors of '77 and '86
        The Haymarket riots
  The armor of labor
    Organization
      Collective action
        Higher wages
        The eight hour day
          The spread of state legislation
    The Knights of Labor
    Stephens and Powderly
    The crisis of 1886
      The decline of the order
  Efforts of the national government
    Methods of arbitration and conciliation
      President Cleveland Compare Volume 44, Pages 128-132
  The rise of the American Federation of Labor
                    Volume 40, Chapter V
    The super-organization of labor
    Associated trade unions
    The annual convention
    Gompers
      Democratic principles

The Story of Labor—Continued
        Diplomatic control
        Lobbyist at Washington
    The menace of the Sherman Anti-Trust Law
      The exemption of labor
        The Clayton Act, 1914   Volume 40, Page 184
    The patriotism of the Federation during the World
      War
      Labor at the Peace Conference
      International labor legislation
The trade union
    The local
      Association of fellow workers
      Adaptation to shifting industrial lines
    Aggressive personalities
      John Mitchell and the United Mine Workers
        The strike of 1902
        The part of President Roosevelt
            Compare Volume 47, Pages 115–120
Railroad brotherhoods   Volume 40, Chapter VII
    Engineers
      Solidarity and statesmanship
        Strict standards of membership
      Success with the collective contract
        Boards of adjustment
      Care of the individual
        Insurance and pensions
      The dispute of 1912
        The Eastern railroads
        The strike threat
        The board of arbitration
          Its decision
            The supremacy of public interest
            The dissent of labor
      Conductors, Firemen, and Trainmen
        Efficient leadership
      The coup of 1916   Compare Volume 38, Pages 236–241
        The swing of the pendulum
          Strike threats of the Brotherhoods

The Story of Labor—Continued
              Demands for increased pay
              Hours of labor involved
           The refusal of arbitration by the Brotherhoods
         The action of the government
           The compliance of President Wilson with the
            insistence of the Brotherhoods
           Forced legislation by Congress
             The Adamson law
               Validated by the Supreme Court
      Government management of the railroads
       A war measure
       McAdoo's readjustment of wages
      Proposals of the Brotherhoods
       The Plumb plan
        Government ownership
        Joint operation
Contentions and methods   Volume 40, Chapter VII
  Standard wage rates
   Collective trade agreements
  The closed shop
   Strikes, picketing, and boycott
    Military organization
    War chests
  Dangers of lawlessness
   Dynamite and murder
  The union label
   The co-operation of trade unions
  Restriction of output
   Rules governing a day's work
   Opposition to piece work
  "Government by injunction"   "   " Pages 252–256
   Reactionary courts
   Deprivation of liberty
    Jury trial
The Reds   "   " Chapter IX
  Syndicalism in Europe
  Floating labor in America
   Ripeness for radicalism

The Story of Labor—Continued
>   The Western Federation of Miners
>   Violence and outrage
>   Forerunner of the "I. W. W."
>   The Industrial Workers of the World
>   The liability of the American Federation of Labor
>   Visions of world conquest
>   A new social order
>   Haywood
>   The Lawrence strike in 1912
>   The army of the unemployed, 1914
>   New York City
>   Public reaction
>   Force met with force
>   Expulsion of the "I. W. W." from cities in
>   Washington
>   Activities during the World War
>   Opposition to war
>   Draft evasion
>   Local vigilantes
>   Conspiracy
>   The Espionage Act

American labor in politics   Volume 40, Chapter XI
>   Early failures
>   The working men's parties of the thirties
>   The National Labor Union of 1866
>   The Labor Reform party of 1872
>   Its national convention
>   The overshadowing Greenback movement, 1876–1884
>   The "venerable Peter Cooper"
>   The hero, General J. B. Weaver
>   The "lurid Ben Butler"
>   Ephemeral labor parties
>   Tax Reformers, Anti-Monopolists, Homesteaders
>   Henry George
>   A meteor across the horizon of labor
>   A new alliance with Western farmers
>   The Populist party, 1892
>   Labor tickets in state campaigns

The Story of Labor—Continued
    Chinese labor in California, 1877
      Kearneyism
   The rise of the Socialist party
    The Socialist Labor convention, 1892
    Debs and the Social-Democrats, 1900
     Candidate again in 1904 and 1908
    Increasing local power
     Berger and Milwaukee
    Ill repute in the World War
   The opposition of the American Federation to a labor party
    Preference for a whip hand over the old parties
     Gompers and the lobby
      Congressmen and the labor vote
    The present grievance
     The open shop and injunctions

Immigration   Volume 35, Pages 141–146
  The third stream of German immigrants
   The change after 1870
    The Prussian air
    The German press
     The Fatherland idolized
    The German vote in the United States
     The interest of the Kaiser
 Homesteaders   Volume 35, Chapter VII
  Scandinavian settlers in the Northwest
  Bohemians in the Mississippi valley
  Poles and Finns
 Urban hordes   Volume 35, Chapter VIII
  Slavs, Lithuanians, Magyars
   Fuel for American mills
  Jews
   Bankers, peddlers, garment makers
   Recruits for radicalism
  Italians, North and South
   Colonies in large cities
    Outdoor laborers

Immigration—Continued
    Greeks
      Confectioners and bootblacks
    Portuguese
      Factory hands in New England
      Gardeners in California
    Armenians and Syrians
      The trader at the front door
   The meeting ground of West and East

                        Volume 35, Chapter IX
      The Chinese in California   Compare Volume 44, Page 31
                                Volume 46, Page 224
                    Volume 40, Pages 238–242
        Coolie labor for gold mines and railroads
        The hostility of American labor
          Recent Americans from Ireland
            Dennis Kearney
        The Burlingame Treaty
          The Angell Mission
          Chinese exclusion acts
      The Jap in America   Volume 46, Pages 235–237
        The rage of Californians
          Alien land bills
        Japanese-American agreements
          Restrictions upon emigration of labor
      Hindoos and Afghans
  Racial infiltration   Volume 35, Chapter X
      Rejected or abandoned lands
        The peasant's instinct
      The Italian and the Slav
        Louisiana, Texas, and California
        Virginia, New England, and the Northwest
          Worn out plantations
          Cut over timber lands
      The transformation of factory centers
        Lawrence, Massachusetts
        Johnstown, Pennsylvania
    New factory towns
      Gary and Whiting, Indiana

Immigration—Continued
  Mining villages
  The American policy   Volume 35, Chapter XI
    Early welcome
    Waves of anti-foreign feeling
      The Alien and Sedition Acts of 1798
      The Know-nothing party of the fifties
      The American Protective Association, 1896
    Immigration laws
      The law of 1819
      The law of 1882
        Selective immigration
      The exclusion of contract labor, 1885
      The law of 1891
        Federal control
        Excluded classes
      Lodge's bill of 1896
        The literacy test
        Veto by President Cleveland
      The law of 1903
        Comprehensive regulation
      The law of 1907
        Roosevelt's interest
        The Immigration Commission
      Contests over the literacy law
        Taft's veto
        Wilson's two vetos
          Passage over his second vetoes
        The law of 1917
          Exclusion, the dominant idea

The Disappearance of the Frontier
  The cattle kings   Volume 26, Chapter VIII
    Indian reservations
    Northward trails
      Moving cattle herds
        Cow towns
          The law of the vigilantes
        Cattle markets

The Disappearance of the Frontier—Continued
          The Chicago stock-yards
     Barbed wire fences and cattle associations
  The arrival of the homesteader   Volume 26, Chapter IX
    The vanguard of settlement
      The end of the cattle range
    The hand of the government
      Removal of illegal inclosures, 1885
        The doom of the cattle ranch
      The Dawes Act of 1887
        The allotment of Indian lands
        The rush into Oklahoma
    Railroads and land booms
      Kansas in 1886
        Wildcat irrigation schemes
    War between sheepherder and cowman
      The Wyoming dead line
    Large scale farming
      Wheat
      The one-crop country
    The Canadian frontier
      Lure for the restless American

The Story of the Farmer
  The ground-swell of discontent   Volume 45, Chapter II
    Over production following the Civil War
      Declining prices of farm products
    The blight of mortgages
    The effect of high protective tariffs
    Dependence upon railroad transportation
      World markets
  The panic of 1873   Compare Volume 38, Pages 157–222
                                 Volume 40, Page 66
    The desperation of the farmer
      High rates of interest
      High costs of transportation
    Hatred of corporations
      The monopoly of railroads
  The weapon of the farmer   Volume 45, Chapters I, III

The Story of the Farmer—Continued
  Collective action
    The grange
      Its social and secret organization
      Its program
        Agricultural education
        Co-operative marketing
        War on monopolies
    The grange in politics
      State legislatures
        Grange laws   Compare Volume 38, Pages 222-229
        Anti-monopoly
      Granger politicians
      Taylor and Donnelly
  The attack upon the railroads   Volume 45, Chapter IV
                    Compare Volume 38, Pages 228-238
    Producer versus non-producer
    Western farmer against Eastern magnate
    The railroad lobby
      State legislatures
    Railroad rate laws
      Public servants or private enterprises?
      The struggle in Illinois
        Maximum fares
        Freight charges based upon distance
        The state railroad commission
          Munn versus Illinois
          The public interest upheld
      Partial success of the railroads
        Manipulation of service
        The problem of interstate traffic
          The way cleared for the Federal Interstate
            Commerce Commission
          The Wabash case
  The failure of the grange   Volume 45, Chapter V
    Unsound growth
      Half-hearted adherents
    Unstable organization
      Inclusion of disloyal elements

The Story of the Farmer—Continued

  Impractical co-operative schemes
   Dislike of the middle man
   Failures in attempts to manufacture farming
    implements
   Bankruptcy
  Achievements of the grange
   Better understanding between farmer and manu-
    facturer
   Social and intellectual stimulus
    The educative value of grange meetings
    Farm journals and newspapers
 The lure of currency inflation   Volume 45, Chapter VI
  The place of the farmer in the Greenback movement
 Increasing distress in the eighties and nineties
           Volume 45, Chapter VII
  The downward trend of prices
   Agricultural products
  Mortgages and taxes
  Rapacious railroads
 The return to collective action Volume 45, Chapter VIII
  Farmers' Alliances: secret societies
   Born of necessity
    Beginnings in Texas
     Ventures in business
     Activity in politics
  The Agricultural Wheel
  Union with the Alliance
   A Southern organization
    Lingering sectional feeling
  The Northwestern Alliance
   Co-operative grain elevators
   Political action
  Attempts at union
  Rapid decline before a rising political party
   The Populist movement

The Construction of a New South
 A new structure from old materials Volume 42, Chapter I

The Construction of a New South—Continued
  The effect of vindictive altruism
    "Reconstruction"
      Its hindrance of industrial development
        The false position of the freedman
      The stupor of defeat dispelled
        The struggle for the supremacy of the white
          man   Volume 42, Chapter II
    The victory of the Confederate soldier
      The "Solid South"
        Republican islands in a Democratic sea
          Unionist mountaineers
            Descendants of Jacksonian Democrats
      Elimination of the negro vote
  The staggering burden of debt
    War obligations
    Repudiation
    Extravagances of the carpetbag government
                Volume 42, Pages 227–233
  The rule of "rebel brigadiers"
    Unreconstructed emotions
      Rejection of Federal aid for education
    The rising generation
The revolt of the middle class   Volume 42, Chapter III
  Common cause with the Westerner
    The difficulty of co-operation
      The presence of the negro
  Granges and Alliances
    Separate organizations
  The place of cotton
    The high price immediately following the Civil War
      The salvation of the South
    Declining prices in the eighties and nineties
      The index of agrarian discontent in the South
        Growing hostility toward the "Money
        Power"
      Wall Street
The rejection of old Confederate leaders
  The overthrow of the "old families"

The Construction of a New South—Continued

 The triumph of Tillman in South Carolina, 1890
  A revolution in the South
   The common man in power
  A struggle primarily within the Democratic party
   The Republican party disgraced
   Constant fear of negro participation in politics
    Populism in the South
     A menace to white supremacy
      Division of the Democratic party
    Elaborated devices of disfranchisement
     Poll taxes
     Literacy tests
      Discrimination
     Residence requirements
     Disqualifying crimes
     Grandfather clauses
      The decision of the Supreme Court, 1915
       The Oklahoma Case
    The popularity of prohibition
    Fear of the negro
 The predicament of the farmer   Volume 42, Chapter **IV**
  Economic slavery
   The "crop lien" and chattel mortgage
    The country merchant as the farmer's banker
     The strangle hold of credit
     Store accounts
   The tenant system
    Farming on shares
   Virtual peonage for the negro
   The brighter side
    A large percentage of land under cultivation by
     the owner
    Agricultural colleges and experiment stations
     The county demonstrator
     Corn and canning clubs
    Improvement of roads
     Rural telephones
     Agricultural journals

The Construction of a New South—Continued
>> The Federal Farm Loan Act, 1910
>>> Removal of mortgages
> Industrial development   Volume 42, Chapter V
>> Ante-bellum manufactures
>>> The destructive effects of the Civil War
>> Renewed activity in textile mills
>>> Southern Expositions in the eighties
>>>> Atlanta and New Orleans
>> Northern investments
>>> Southern savings, the greater part of the new capital
>> The progress of North Carolina in cotton manufacture
>>> A leader among Southern states
>>> Second only to Massachusetts
>> Cotton seed products
>>> Salad oil
>>> Fertilizer
>> Lumbering
>>> Louisiana, Mississippi, and North Carolina
>> The iron industry
>>> Birmingham, Alabama
>> Tobacco
>>> The American Tobacco Company
>>>> North Carolina
> Labor in the South   Volume 42, Chapter VI
>> Textile operatives
>>> The movement of families from farm to mill village
>>>> Child labor
>>> The rural attitude
>>>> Agricultural environment
>>>> Sterile soil for the labor agitator
>>>>> Little interest in organized labor
>> Workers in tobacco factories
>>> The replacement of the negro by machinery
>>>> White operators
>> The wage system
>>> The day's pay
>>> Piece work
>> The place of the negro

The Construction of a New South—Continued
  Hardest, least pleasant tasks
  The race problem   Volume 42, Chapter VII
   The negro, a black Saxon?
    The Southern view
     The negro, an inferior
   The negro in the South
    Agriculturist and domestic servant
    The Southern color line
     Work beside white women
    The slow advance of education of the negro
  The northward migration
  The northern reception
  Disillusionment of the negro
  The white man's nameless dread
   Booker T. Washington's plan to prevent the explosion
   Economic independence for the negro
   His enemies
    Negro "intellectuals"
     Social aspirations
    The lowest third of the white community
     A vicious sense of superiority
   The great necessity
    A change in human nature
     Admission of racial equality in the American
     political and social system
  Education in the South   Volume 42, Chapter VIII
   Public schools since the Civil War
    The blight of reconstruction
    Negro schools
   Restoration of Southern control
    Separate schools
    Reaction from carpetbag extravagance
   The Peabody Fund
    Northern philanthropy
    Southern apathy
     Private education for the few
     Distrust of education for the negro
  Booker T. Washington and the negro

The Construction of a New South—Continued
    Hampton
    Tuskegee
      Industrial training
   The recent spread of public education
    High schools
  Southern colleges
    Revival of old institutions
    Vanderbilt University
    Growing denominational colleges
The South of today   Volume 42, Chapter IX
   Dying prejudices
    Occupations befitting gentlemen
  Waning traditions
    The leadership of the planters
  Changing standards
    Prohibition
    The Sabbath
  Social ferment
    Disappearance of the Southern colonel
    Arrival of the business woman
    The code of honor

The Development of Education
  Technical training
    Beginnings before the Civil War   Volume 33, Chapter XIV
    The effect of the Morrill Act
      Agricultural colleges   "   "   XV
  Higher education for women   "   "   XVI
    Girls' schools
    Women's colleges
    Co-education in the West
  Catholic education   "   "   XIII
    Franciscan missions
    Jesuit colleges
    Parochial schools
  Innovations and reforms   "   "   XVII
    Sheldon and Alcott
    The Quincy experiment

The Development of Education—Continued
    The Gary system
    The university of today   Volume 33, Chapter XVIII
      Expanding curricula
      Athletics and fraternities
      Extension courses
      Missionaries of American education
        Turkey and China

The Literature of the New Union   Volume 34, Chapter X
    The span of a lifetime
    The work of Howells
  "The Second Discovery of America"
    Mark Twain, observer
    Bret Harte, prospector
    Jack London's West
      Alaska
    The Scotsmen, Miller and Muir
    Southern writers
      Harris and Page
    James Whitcomb Riley
    The "abandoned farm" of New England
  Henry James
    Child of America
    Citizen of England
  Stedman, Gilder, and Aldrich
  The American short story
    O. Henry
  Writers of nature study
    Burroughs

CHAPTER XVIII

THE NEW SECTIONALISM

THE Civil War left the Republican party in complete control of the national government. The Democrats were discredited by secession in the South and opposition to the war in the North. Furthermore, the Southern whites were disfranchised. As the negroes had been given the vote they had been herded into the ranks of the Republicans. Enjoying the prestige of military victory, the party of Lincoln could look forward to a long lease of power at Washington. Its security in power, however, was one of its greatest dangers.

From the idealism of the war period Republican leaders plunged into the vindictiveness of reconstruction. By giving the negro the vote, they created a "Solid South" in opposition. Moreover, as industrialism developed, manufacturers and railroad builders had favors to ask of the

politician both state and national. They naturally approached the party in power. Big business
became intimately allied with the Republican
party. Agrarian groups watched this rapprochement with misgivings. Politics like all other
phases of American life were making adjustments
to the new order.

The most striking of these was the intricate
development of the party machine and the rising
power of the political boss. More and more the
opportunities of business drew the best men away
from competition for public office. They did not,
however, abandon politics but exerted their influence through dealing with the boss and his
organization. As a result, the class of professional
politicians grew in number and importance. The
sustaining force of the party machine was the
material reward which faithful service could en-
sure. These were sometimes profitable contracts
but more often offices in the civil service of the
state or nation. The henchmen of the party in
power lived on the fruits of victory. Opponents
hoped for the day when their turn would come.
The corruption which came to the surface in
Grant's administration and continued vindictiveness toward the South brought inevitable reaction.

Liberal Republicans broke with the organization of their party in 1872 and centered their attack upon the "spoils system." Western farmers also wavered in their Republican allegiance. They believed that the party was granting undue favors to Northern manufacturers and Eastern railroad capitalists. Protective tariffs, high freight rates, and a contracting currency all seemed to be designed for the benefit of the North and East. Agrarian parties from the West, therefore, entered national politics and sought alliances with Eastern laborers and fellow farmers in the South. A new sectionalism had appeared. But, one after another, the parties of protest met failure. The machine remained unshaken. The connection between business and politics grew closer.

For a quarter century, from 1861 to 1885, the Republican party held the presidency. Within its ranks the struggle between the liberals and the organization continued. When President Garfield was assassinated by a disappointed office-seeker, the machine gave way to the demand for civil service reform. But, in many respects, Republican policy was unsound. Divisions within the party widened. In 1884, a reformer from the North led the Democrats to victory.

For twelve years Cleveland remained a central figure on the political stage. Although imbued with liberal ideas, he was also sympathetic with the point of view of business. In his first administration, he advocated a lower tariff to eliminate surplus revenues, stopped short pension abuses, studied carefully the wave of violence and social unrest of 1886, and approved a regulation of railroads by a federal Interstate Commerce Commission. But he flatly refused to ally himself with the Western farmers who, as their financial distress increased, clamored for the expansion of the currency by the free coinage of silver. The times were chaotic. Cleveland was swept from power in 1888 by the Republican, Harrison. The Republicans promptly revised the tariff to increase protection, widened the scope of the pension law, and voted to spend the national surplus on the improvement of rivers and harbours. They sought to win Western support with the Sherman Silver Purchase Act and the Sherman Anti-Trust Law. They abandoned a "Force Bill" directed against Southern disenfranchisement of the negro. Nevertheless, a popular revolt overthrew Harrison. Cleveland returned to power.

Cleveland's second administration marked a

pause on the eve of a great battle. The Panic of
1893 and the labor troubles which followed dis-
arranged political plans. Cleveland antagonized
the West by forcing the repeal of the Sherman
Silver Act to meet the necessities of the treasury.
He returned to tariff reform only to receive from
his own party a bill so full of protectionist jobbery
that in disgust he allowed it to become a law without his signature. He angered labor by sending
federal troops to Chicago to protect the mails in
the Pullman strike. But amid all the troubles
that beset his administration he held firm to his
refusal to cheapen American currency by per-
mitting the free coinage of silver. His reward
came in 1896 when he was repudiated by his own
party and ridiculed by Republicans.

In that year the forces of the West which had
been uniting in the Populist party were captured
for the Democratic party by the maneuvers of
William Jennings Bryan. The protest of the
West was genuine. The farmers perceived real
evils; but they chose a remedy which most business men and most men of education believed to
be wrong. The Republican party, working under
the masterly direction of Mark Hanna, convinced
the great middle class of small investors, that free

silver was an economic fallacy and held before laborers the vision of a "full dinner pail." McKinley was elected. The problem of a readjustment of political methods went over to the Twentieth Century for solution.

Behind President McKinley "Big Business" controlled the national administration. Hanna in the Senate and Reed in the House drew the reins of power into their hands. In short order, the Dingley tariff was rushed through both houses. Protectionism flowered with favors for special interests. After the war with Spain, the Gold Standard Act forever laid to rest the turbulent spirit of free silver and bimetallism. At the end of his administration McKinley faced Bryan in a campaign which centered in questions of foreign policy. Should the United States assume the burdens and responsibilities of a colonial empire?

The Effect of War upon Republicanism Volume 43, Chapter III
  Corroding vindictiveness
    The obliteration of Lincoln's idealism
    Black Republicans
      "The bloody shirt"
  The odor of commercialism
    Capture of the Republican party
    Scandals in high offices   Volume 45, Page 12

The Effect of War upon Democracy
  The stigma of opposition to the war   Volume 45, Pages 11–12

The Effect of War upon Democracy—Continued

The white man's party in the South   Volume 43, Page 14

                              Volume 42, Chapter II

    "The Solid South"

    Reaction against Reconstruction

Grantism in Power

The aftermath of war   Volume 43, Chapter III

                Compare Volume 38, Pages 125–129

    Corruption and official immorality

       The Credit Mobilier

          Congressmen and the Union Pacific

       The Whiskey Ring

          Revenue officers and distillers

       Belknap, Secretary of War

          Graft at Indian posts

    The observations of Senator Hoar

The natural outcome in the South   Volume 32, Chapter XIII

    Grant's changes of policy

       The Amnesty Act, 1872

The favored section

    Northern manufactures   Volume 45, Pages 14, 20

       Protective tariffs

    Northern finance

       Railroad manipulation   Compare Volume 38, Pages 71–89

       The re-establishment of the currency Volume 45, Page 83

          The resumption of specie payment

Stirrings of Protest

The Liberal Republican movement   Volume 45, Chapter II

    Purposes:

       Administrative reform

       Lenience to the South

    The candidacy of Horace Greeley

    The failure of the alliance with the Democrats

The agrarian parties   Volume 45, Chapter III

    Grievances of the western farmers

       Railroad rates   "   "   IV

       Farmer legislation

The Greenback party   "   "   VI

Stirrings of Protest—Continued
>   Demand for an expanding currency
>   The paper money of the Civil War
>   Opposition to the resumption of specie payment
>   Support of the Bland-Allison Silver Act, 1878
>   The alliance of western farmers and eastern laborers
>   The unrest of the working men
>   The National Labor Party of 1872
>   Greenback candidates
>   Peter Cooper in 1876
>   Gen. J. B. Weaver in 1880
>   Ben Butler in 1884

The Turning Point of 1876   Volume 32, Pages 294–302
>   Revival of war hatreds
>   Blaine and the "bloody shirt"
>   The rival candidates
>   Hayes and Tilden
>   The disputed election
>   The device
>   An electoral commission
>   "The great steal"
>   The selection of Hayes
>   The gentlemen's agreement
>   The end of Northern domination over the South
>   The predicament of President Hayes
>   The dilemma in the South   Volume 44, Chapter I
>   Tolerance for the Confederate or protection for
>   the negro
>   Sound money or adequate currency
>   Hayes' veto of the Bland-Allison bill Volume 45, Page 158
>   The resumption of specie payment   "   "   Page 83
>   Rising industrial unrest   "   "   Page 88
>   Compare Volume 40, Chapter IV
>   The strikes of 1877
>   The use of Federal troops
>   Rewards to partisans or civil service reform
>   Volume 43, Pages 139–140
>   Hayes' removal of Arthur and Cornell

The Growth of Party Machines
The foundations   Volume 43, Chapter IV
  Municipal mechanisms
    The opportunity of the boss
      Public utilities as private playthings
                   Compare Volume 39, Chapter V
    Jobs for loyal vote-getters
      Ward heelers and immigrants
      Somnolent citizens
A typical machine
  Tammany Hall   Volume 43, Chapter V
    Its early origin
      Aaron Burr
      William Mooney
        "Trifles for Mrs. Mooney"
      Swartwout, Jacksonian
        Defaulter in public office
    The reign of Tweed
      His Ring
      The public benefactors
      Jennings and Nast
    Kelley and Croker
    Tammany's scientific organization
      The general committee
        The executive committee
      The district leader
        His lieutenants
      The house-to-house canvass
        The lubricant
          Offices, jobs, favors, and charity
Lesser oligarchies   Volume 43, Chapter VI
  Philadelphia's Gas Ring
  Butler, boss of St. Louis
    The reformer Folk
  Cox and Cincinnati
  Gang politics in San Francisco
    Ruef and Schmitz
  "Doc" Ames and Minneapolis
  Reform

The Growth of Party Machines—Continued

State legislatures, party tools   Volume 43, Chapter VII
  The legislative caucus
  Electoral districting
    The gerrymander
  Elections of United States Senators
  Legislation
    Favoritism
      Charters and lobbyists
    Blackmail
      Special interests
  The power of the boss
    Tammany and Governor Sulzer
    The Quay Machine in Pennsylvania
Partisan power at Washington   Volume 43, Chapter VIII
  The place of the President
    The puppet of party managers?
  The Speaker of the House
    Czar Reed and the rules
      Committees
    Cannonism
      The insurgents of 1910
  "Senatorial courtesy"
    Party chieftains   Volume 44, Pages 18–24
      "Big Business"
    The control of appointments
      A whiphand over the President   Volume 43, Page 140
Reforms   "   Chapter IX
  State control of elections
    The Australian ballot
  Anti-lobby laws
    The leadership of Massachusetts
  Initiative and referendum
  Government by commission
    City managers
  Primary laws   "   "   X
    Party lists
    Enrollment books
    Central Committees

The Growth of Party Machines—Continued
    State supervision
    Candidates and platforms
      The "Crawford County Plan"
    Corrupt Practices Acts
    Citizen's tickets
      Fusion candidates

Civil Service Reform   Volume 43, Chapter XI
  Beginnings under Grant
    Previous views of office-holding
      John Adams
      Jefferson
      Jackson
        "The Spoils System"
      The predicament of Lincoln
    Pioneers
      Jenckes and Schurz
    Grant and the Commission of 1871
      G. W. Curtis
      Failure
  Hayes and the Republican machine Volume 43, Pages 139–140
    The removal of Cornell and Arthur
    The activity of the Civil Service Reform League
      Private stimulus to public opinion
  Garfield, Arthur, and the Pendleton Act
                   Volume 43, Pages 140–142
    Garfield's defiance of the New York bosses
    The effect of Garfield's assassination Volume 44, Pages 21–22
    The machine politician as President
    Arthur's support of the Pendleton Act, 1883
  Cleveland, Harrison, and the civil service
                  Volume 44, Pages 109–112
    Cleveland's extension of the system
    Roosevelt as Harrison's commissioner
                  Volume 47, Chapter III

The Return of Democracy to Power
  The miscarriage of Republican policy   Volume 44, Chapter I
    The negro in the South

The Return of Democracy to Power—Continued
    The end of force bills
  Weaknesses in Congressional government
  Division within Republican ranks
    The election of 1880
    "Stalwarts" against "Half-Breeds"
      Garfield, Blaine, and Conkling
  The impotence of Arthur's administration

Volume 44, Chapter II

    Congressional blundering
      Lawlessness in the West
        Jesse James
      Chinese immigration
      Mormon polygamy
      Pork-barrel appropriations
      The tariff of 1883
        Sectional interests
    Presidential vetoes
  The opportunity of Democracy
    The wave of discontent with party leadership

Cleveland's First Administration
  Cleveland's victory over Blaine, 1884 Volume 44, Chapter III
    His previous career
      Sheriff, mayor, and governor
        New York State
    "Mugwump" Republicans
    "Rum, Romanism, and Rebellion"
      Blaine's campaign in New York
        The deciding state
  The restoration of Presidential supremacy

Volume 44, Chapter IV

    Senatorial encroachment
      Approval of appointments
      The repeal of the Tenure of Office Act
  The atrophy of the House   Volume 44, Chapter V
    The decline of control over legislation
      The standing committees
    The clique dominating the House
      The Committee on Appropriations

Cleveland's First Administration—Continued
    The deadening effect of faction
      Contesting Democrats
        Randall and Morrison
    The rise of the Speaker
Cleveland's appointments   Volume 44, Chapter VI
  The enforcement of the civil service law
    Democratic wrath
  The Chief Justice of the Supreme Court
    Senatorial obstruction
Cleveland and Northern sentimentality
  Pension abuses
    Presidential vetoes
The problem of the surplus and the tariff
  Cleveland's message to Congress, 1887
    "A condition, not a theory"
    A demand for revision of tariff laws
  The Mills Bill
    Acceptance by the House
    Delay in the Senate
      The issue in the election of 1888
Social unrest   Volume 44, Chapter VII
  The Knights of Labor and violence
    Railroad strikes, 1886
    The Haymarket Riot, 1886
  Measures of the Cleveland administration
    Congressional investigation
    Presidential proposals
      Senatorial obstruction
    The Department of Labor
  The Socialist movement
    The foreign element
      The taint of anarchy
      The Haymarket affair
    The recoil of organized labor
      The American Federation of Labor
  The reformer, Henry George
    Labor candidate for mayor of New York
  The agrarian protest

Cleveland's First Administration—Continued
      Hatred of the money power
      Demand for an expanded currency
        Coinage of silver
        The resistance of Cleveland's administration
     "Third parties" in the election of 1888
    Railroads and the public interest
                         Compare Volume 38, Chapter XII
  The Wabash decision   "   " Pages 232–233
  The Interstate Commerce Act
  Cleveland's approval

The Harrison Interlude   Volume 44, Chapter VIII
  The peculiar power of the Republican machine
    Control of President, Senate, and House
    Czar Reed, Speaker of the House
  The Republican method of eliminating a surplus
    The "Billion-Dollar Congress"
      The pension bill
        Corporal Tanner's bounty
      Rivers and harbors
        Extravagant appropriations
      The McKinley Tariff
        Protection of American industry
        Reduction of the surplus
        Blaine and reciprocity
  The Sherman Anti-Trust Act
    Compulsory competition
      Checks upon "Big Business"
  The Sherman Silver Act
    The coinage of silver bullion
                      Compare Volume 45, Pages 159–160
    The danger of a stampede to free coinage
      Party discipline
    Democratic opposition
  Abandonment of a new "Force Bill"
                         Compare Volume 42, Page 48
    Disfranchisement of the negro completed
    Removal of Southern obstruction to the tariff act

The Harrison Interlude—Continued
  Popular revolt against the Republican policy
    Protection and profiteering
      The Republican boss of the House, 1890
    Harrisonian complacency
      Blaine's personal aversion
  The campaign of 1892
    Harrison or Blaine?
      The renomination of Harrison
    The Democratic renomination of Cleveland
      The factious opposition of Hill and New York
      Cleveland's fearless resistance to free silver
    The People's Party
    The effect of the Homestead Strike
    The success of the people's candidate, Cleveland

Cleveland's Second Administration   Volume 44, Chapter IX
  The Panic of 1893
    The effect of the silver act upon the Treasury
      The vanishing gold reserve
    The crash in the business world
      The National Cordage Company
      The Philadelphia and Reading Railroad
      Bank failures
        Distress in the West and South
    Cleveland's demand for repeal of the silver act
      Persistent office seekers
        Cleveland's illness
      Cleveland's pressure upon Congress
        The repeal
  The dilemma of the Treasury
    The endless chain
      The gold reserve
    Cleveland's arrangement with Morgan
    Complicating foreign affairs
      The British-Venezuelan dispute
        The insistence of Cleveland
          The Monroe Doctrine
    Cleveland's failure to meet the popular grievance

Cleveland's Second Administration—Continued
      An inadequate currency supply
  Tariff reform   Volume 44, Chapter X
    The Wilson bill
    The Senate and the interests
      Quay's methods of obstruction
      Gorman's compromise
      Cleveland's disgust
    An investigation
      Havemeyer and the Sugar Trust
  The grievances of working men
    The armies of Kelley, Frye, and Coxey
    The Pullman strike
      Debs and injunctions
      Cleveland and the United States mails
      Governor Altgeld and states rights
  Fellow Democrats with Cleveland
    Senator Hill of New York
      Appointments to the Supreme Court
    Congressman Bryan
      Attacks upon Cleveland
  The fate of the income tax
    A provision of the Wilson-Gorman Tariff
    The adverse decision of the Supreme Court

Free Silver and Populism
  Successors of the Greenback and Granger movements
                       Volume 45, Chapter IX
    The union of labor parties and farmers' alliances
      The contest of sections
        South and West against North and East
          Agriculture versus manufacturing
          Common man versus capitalist
  Dissatisfaction with the Silver Act of 1890
    The demand for "free silver"
      Hardships of the debtor class
    The appearance of People's Parties
      The congressional elections
        Remonstrance against the Republican tariff

Free Silver and Populism—Continued

        Mrs. Lease and "Sockless Jerry" Simpson

           The wrath of Kansas farmers

      Populists sent to Congress

    The union of parties of discontent

The trial of strength in 1892   Volume 45, Chapter X

    The candidacy of J. B. Weaver

      The platform: Grievances of the common man

  Inroads upon the older parties

  A million ballots

  Twenty-two electoral votes

The check of the panic of '93   Volume 44, Chapter IX

                           Volume 45, Page 104

  The repeal of the Silver Act

  Distress in the South and West

The returning tide of Populism   Volume 45, Chapter XI

  The silver issue

    Origins

      The "Ohio Idea," of 1868

      The "Crime of '73"

      The Bland-Allison Act of 1878

    The theory of bimetallism

    International negotiations

    Mining interests

      Interplay with the needs of the debtor West

        Sherman Act of 1890

  The union of Free Silver and Populism

    The struggle with Republicanism in Kansas, 1893

    Uncertainties in the congressional elections of 1894

      An increased popular vote

      Losses in Western states

        The failure of fusion

  The approach of '96

    The presidential year

    Negotiations with Republicans and Democrats

      Cleveland's stamp upon Democracy

                       Volume 44, Pages 118-120

        The split

      Republican leanings toward Cleveland's position

The Election of 1896   Volume 45, Chapter XII
                        Compare Volume 44, Pages 218–220
  Hanna and Republican maneuvers
    The safe candidate, McKinley
    The tariff, the "full dinner pail," and then the gold
        standard
      The bolt of silver Republicans
  Bryan, both Democrat and Populist
    Tillman's condemnation of Cleveland
    Bryan's address to the Democratic convention
      His nomination endorsed by Populists
  The campaign
    McKinley's speeches from the "front porch"
    Bryan's tours
      The success of McKinley
  The death of Populism
    Its bequest to the Twentieth Century
                              Volume 45, Chapter XIII

        Progressivism
        Farm blocs
        The Non-partisan League

McKinley as President
  The power of Hanna and Reed
  The Dingley Tariff, 1897
    Protection in full bloom
  The Gold Standard Act, 1900

CHAPTER XIX

THE PUBLIC INTEREST PARAMOUNT

In the first decade of the Twentieth Century, the sectional movements which had agitated American politics since the Civil War merged into a nation-wide demand that the public interest be served and that the particular desires of individuals, classes, or sections be subordinated to the welfare of the whole. America had achieved an economic and social integration never known before. Business and politics had drawn together in close alliance. Party machines had concentrated political power. Nevertheless, the movements of protest did not die; they came to fruition. The remonstrances of farmers and laborers which had created the Populist party grew into the wider Progressive movement. Roosevelt sensed the trend of public opinion and brought his administration into harmony with it. He undertook to regulate "Big Business" and gave a vitality to

the Sherman Anti-Trust Law that few had believed possible. He took the same strong middle ground in his management of labor. Reclamation of waste lands and conservation of national resources were obviously for the benefit of all and an obligation of the present to future generations.

Roosevelt's successor continued to maintain the public interest as superior to all others, but Taft, like Cleveland before him, was harassed by strife within his party. The contest between the Congressional insurgents and conservative Republicans became bitter with the overthrow of Speaker Cannon's rule over the House of Representatives. Both sides prepared to fight for control of the party convention in 1912. The conservatives won. Progressives bolted the party, and the Democrats had their opportunity. Wilson, nominated because of his liberal tendencies, was elected.

During the first two years of Wilson's administration a spirit of liberalism prevailed. The movement of protest bore fruit in a series of reform laws that had never been equalled in the history of the nation. The World War deflected public attention to foreign affairs, but the American people followed their President with extraordinary unanimity into war, enlarging their devotion to the

public interest into determination to "make the world safe for democracy." The movement for reform in America grew into a movement for international reform. Then came the Armistice, the Treaty of Versailles, the quarrel between the President and the Senate, bitterness and disillusionment. The significance of all that has happened, only the future can make clear.

The Figure of Roosevelt
  Early years   Volume 47, Chapter I
    Harvard and Dakota
  Politics as a career   "   "   II
    Tenements and cigar-makers
    A regular Republican
      His support of Blaine
  Public service   "   "   III
    Candidate for Mayor of New York
    Civil Service Commissioner
      President Harrison's Cabinet
    Police Commissioner of New York   "   "   IV
    Assistant Secretary of the Navy   "   "   XV
      Colonel of Rough Riders
    Governor of New York   "   "   V
      Platt's machine
      The independence of Roosevelt
  The Presidency   "   "   VI
    The election of 1900
    A sidetrack for the Governor of New York
                   Volume 47, Chapter IV
      McKinley's running mate
    Imperialism and Free Silver
      Bryan's campaign
    The assassination of McKinley

The Figure of Roosevelt—Continued
>   Roosevelt's effort to continue McKinley's policy
>   His break with machine-politicians

The Regulation of Big Business   Volume 47, Chapter VII
>   Roosevelt's middle ground
>   Application of the Sherman Anti-Trust Law
>   Dissolution of the Northern Securities Company
>   Compare Volume 39, Chapter VI
>   Volume 38, Chapter VII
>   Prosecution of the Standard Oil and American
>   Tobacco Companies
>   Creation of the Department of Commerce and Labor
>   The Bureau of Corporations
>   The Hepburn Railroad Rate Law of 1906
>   Volume 38, Pages 234–236
>   Rate-making
>   Determination of maximum rates by the Interstate
>   Commerce Commission
>   Extension of the jurisdiction of the Commission
>   The ban upon the rebate
>   Federal prosecutions
>   The Standard Oil case
>   Judge Landis' fine
>   The panic of 1907   Compare Volume 41, Chapter VIII
>   The case of the Tennessee Coal and Iron Company
>   Roosevelt's action
>   Services of the Steel Corporation
>   Pure Food and Meat Inspection Laws, 1906
>   Effects upon business
>   Safeguards to public interest

Labor: Conservative and Radical   Volume 47, Chapter VIII
>   Trade unions and collective bargaining
>   The Anthracite Coal Strike, 1902
>   Compare Volume 40, Pages 129–130
>   Roosevelt and arbitration
>   The eight-hour day and compensation laws
>   The open-shop

Labor: Conservative and Radical—Continued
      Roosevelt and Gompers
  The I. W. W.   Compare Volume 40, Chapter IX
    The bombing episode in Idaho, 1905
      Roosevelt's opinion of Haywood

The National Resources   Volume 47, Chapter IX
  Reclamation and Conservation
    The Newlands Act of 1902
      Irrigation of arid western lands
        Shoshone and Roosevelt Dams
    Forest reserves
      The work of Pinchot
      The National Forest Act, 1905
        Regulated cutting
      The resistance of land grabbers
    The Inland Waterways Commission
      The conference at the White House, 1908
        The National Conservation Commission

Taft's Administration   Volume 47, Chapter XII
  Preparation for the presidency
  Substantial achievements
    Amendments to the Constitution
      The income tax
      Direct election of Senators
    The admission of New Mexico and Arizona
    The parcels post and postal savings banks
    Publicity for campaign contributions
    Extension of the authority of the Interstate Com-
      merce Commission
      Establishment of the Commerce Court
        The Mann-Elkins Act
      Dissolution of the Standard Oil and American
        Tobacco Companies
                  Compare Volume 41, Pages 152–153
                          Volume 39, Pages 53–54
  Tariff fights
    Taft's view of protection

Taft's Administration—Continued

The Payne-Aldrich Law, 1909
The remonstrance of the Middle West
Insurgent Republicans
Taft's speech at Winona
Reciprocity with Canada   Volume 46, Page 246
Taft's success in Congress
Rejection by Canada   Volume 49, Pages 239–252
National patriotism in Canada
Rebuff for "Manifest Destiny"
The Ballinger-Pinchot controversy   Volume 47, Chapter XII

Progressivism

The Insurgents in Congress, 1910
The revolt against Speaker Cannon
Congressional elections, 1910
The effect of a Democratic House
The return of Roosevelt from Africa
Resumption of party leadership
His speech at Ossawattomie, Kansas
"The New Nationalism"
His crusade against the New York machine
The campaign for Stimson
Governor of New York
Defeat
The national campaign of 1912   Volume 47, Chapter XIII
The demand for "Direct Democracy"
Initiative, referendum, and recall
Direct primaries
Popular election of Senators
Woman suffrage
The steam-roller at Chicago
The Republican nomination of Taft
The bolt of the Progressives
The candidacy of Roosevelt
The charge against the Republican convention
Fraudulent management
The religious atmosphere of the Progressive convention

Progressivism—Continued
  "Onward Christian Soldiers"
  Roosevelt's "Confession of Faith"
  The platform
 The opportunity of the Democratic party
         Volume 47, Chapter **XIV**
  Wilson, representative of progressive Democracy
  Election to the Presidency
 The passing of the Progressive party
  The refusal of Roosevelt to lead in 1916
  The choice of Hughes
   The union of Progressive Republicans with the
    Old Guard
  Its stamp upon the Republican party
Wilson's Administration
 Previous career   Volume 48, Chapter **I**
 Democratic legislation
  The Underwood Tariff, 1913
  The Federal Reserve Banking System, 1913
  The Federal Trade Commission, 1914
  The Clayton Anti-Trust Act, 1914 Volume 41, Pages 153–154
         Volume 40, Pages 99–100
         Volume 48, Page 90
  The Philippine Government Act, 1916
       Volume 46, Pages 216–217
  The Farm Loan Act, 1916   Volume 42, Pages 84–85
  The Child Labor Law, 1916
      Compare Volume 40, Pages 249–250
  The Adamson Law, 1916   Volume 40, Pages 163–166
         Volume 41, Pages 236–238
 Liberalism in the Supreme Court
  The appointment of Brandeis

CHAPTER XX

THE NEW RÔLE AS A WORLD POWER

THE end of the War of 1812 was a definite turning point for the American people. Before the Treaty of Ghent they had been much concerned with the affairs of Europe. They had won their independence from the British Empire, but for seventeen years after the Peace of 1783 they were bound to France by the alliance with which they had secured French assistance in the Revolution. As President, Washington chose to hold the United States from participation in the cause of Revolutionary France. The French Alliance was eventually thrown off with the consent of Napoleon, but not until American opinion had been divided and American political parties separated on the issue of foreign sympathies. Finally, the United States was drawn into the European wars that raged about Napoleon. It emerged from its second contest with Great Britain with a fighting record

that was not entirely glorious, but with its territory intact and its economic as well as its political independence assured. After 1815 Americans gave little heed to Europe and concentrated their energies upon building a great nation in a rich continent. The world was formally notified of their intention to guard the western world against further European encroachment and to keep out of European affairs. The Monroe Doctrine of 1823 set up the standard of American isolation.

For three-quarters of a century the citizens of the United States were engrossed in their own national affairs. Expansion to the Pacific, war to preserve the Union, and creation of an industrial civilization in turn demanded the complete attention and the best energy of a vigorous and growing people. Foreign affairs, usually contingent upon national growth, crowded occasionally into the minds of the voters, but it was not until the war with Spain in 1898 that the average citizen ever thought of America in terms of its world relationships or pondered the problems that grow out of membership in the society of nations. Yet before this contest, incidents had occurred which pointed to the later development.

In the Fifties an American naval commander

had opened the ports of Japan. Twenty years after, the United States had taken an interest in the natives of the South Sea Islands and established a claim to the harbor of Pago Pago in Samoa. By the Nineties, American missionary and commercial enterprise in Hawaii had so matured that the foreigners were able to throw off native rule. In the same years, President Cleveland had insisted that the United States must participate in the settlement of a boundary dispute between Great Britain and Venezuela. When he was rebuffed, he offered the alternative of war. To an astonished world, the Monroe Doctrine, sometimes forgotten by Americans themselves in the press of domestic affairs, was reasserted with a vigor that made it the basic determinant in relationships of the western hemisphere. Then came the war with Spain.

The result for the United States of a hundred days of fighting was a chain of possessions reaching from Porto Rico to the Philippines. The United States gradually became conscious of the strategic value of Hawaii, annexed in 1898, as a naval base for the protection of the new imperial domain. A large group of American citizens believed that the acquisitions should not be retained for they held

that imperialism is incompatible with democracy. But the imperialists won the election of 1900. To Roosevelt fell the task of consolidating the empire and planning for its defence. He promptly advocated and secured a stronger navy and made possible the construction and control of the Panama canal, now for the United States more than ever a strategic necessity. Whether or not some Americans decried the trend of the times, the United States had become possessed of an empire. It was in fact a world power with positive interests beyond its own territorial confines. Rising from the new situation were three developments: the American policy in the Caribbean Sea, the peculiar concern of the United States in Asiatic affairs, and the relationship of the United States to world peace conferences at The Hague.

After the United States had acquired possessions in the Caribbean, other states in that region must so order their relations with foreign powers that none would have excuse to land soldiers for the protection of national interests. European or Asiatic troops in the West Indies or Central America might result in the establishment of a base near the Panama canal and jeopardize the whole American plan of defence. This new inter-

pretation of the Monroe Doctrine made the United States policeman of the Caribbean. Pan-Americanism, which had been the professed aim of the United States for relations within the western hemisphere, lost some of its force as a result of distrust. Many Hispanic-Americans saw in it all only Yankee determination to dominate the western continents.

At the opening of the Twentieth Century, China seemed to be on the verge of dissolution and the nations of the world hovering over it like a flock of vultures. American people had long been interested in the work of their Christian missionaries to China. With the acquisition of the Philippines, the American government also perceived that it had an interest in the welfare of the Celestial Empire. Between the rival powers of Europe, the United States interposed the policy of the "open door" backed by American cooperation in the international expeditionary force to punish offenders in the Boxer uprising. China was not dismembered. An accord has grown between the governments at Washington and Peking.

The third development in American relations with the world was the American acceptance of a

place in the peace conferences at The Hague.
The United States became a party to many international commitments to the cause of peaceful
co-operation among the peoples of the world. It
was obvious to careful observers that the tradition-
al American policy of isolation had been modified
materially by the Caribbean and Asiatic policies
and by the presence of American representatives
at The Hague.

The glare of the European conflagration in 1914
sharply outlined the transformation in the situation of the United States. After Germany invaded Belgium, two years and a half elapsed before the American people realized that civilization
was at stake. Germany's use of submarine war-
fare roused the United States to feel that its own
interests were vitally threatened. Then, with an
idealism and unity of purpose never surpassed in
any of its other wars, America threw itself into a
struggle for international reform. The threat of
German militarism was destroyed. When the
conflict was over, however, the old American in-
stinct of isolation reasserted itself. The United
States sent a chill of fear to the hearts of many
European liberals by turning its back on the
League of Nations. Had the "war to end war"

been fought in vain? But the American people can no longer think of isolation in terms of the Nineteenth Century. The United States has interests and commitments over the world, and Americans cannot, if they would, refuse to think in terms of world relationships. The past history of America has been the story of development of national strength surpassing any in the world. The history of the future will be the chronicle of the use of that strength for good or evil on the earth.

The Beginning of a Peculiar Interest in Central and South America
  Basic principles   Volume 46, Chapter I
    The Monroe Doctrine
  The Panama Congress
    The failure of an early Pan-American policy
  Projects for an Isthmian canal   Volume 46, Pages 26-31
    Arrangements with Colombia, 1846
    Arrangements with Mexico, 1853
    British interests in Honduras
      The Mosquito coast
      The Clayton-Bulwer Treaty, 1850
  Blaine's conception of Pan-Americanism
                      Volume 46, Chapter IV
    American mediation in South American disputes
    France and Venezuela
    The French canal company at Panama
    Blaine's effort to annul the Clayton-Bulwer Treaty
    The Pan-American congress, 1889
      Reciprocity
      The Bureau of American Republics

Growing American Interests in the Pacific Volume 46, Chapter III

The purchase of Alaska, 1867

  Seward's negotiations with Russia

    The wave of gratitude

      The fiction of the Russian fleet

Commodore Perry and Japan, 1853   "   "   V

  The introduction of Japan to international society

American participation in the affairs of Samoa, 1872

  The treaty of 1878

  English, German, and American ships of war

    The hurricane of 1889

  International control in Samoa

Hawaii

  Native kings

  Foreign inhabitants

  American missionaries

  The policy of the United States

    Webster's extension of the Monroe Doctrine, 1842

    Marcy's negotiations, 1853

    Blaine's invitation to the Pan-American Congress, 1889

  The revolution of 1893

    American "protection"

    The request for annexation

  Cleveland's reversal of Harrison's policy

  Annexation to the United States, 1898 Volume 46, Page 200

Problems of the United States and Canada

  The Caroline affair   Volume 46, Chapter II

    The boasts of McLeod   Compare Volume 49, Pages 91–92

      American designs on Canada

  The Webster-Ashburton treaty, 1842

    The boundaries of Maine and Nova Scotia

                 Compare Volume 49, Pages 116–121

  Sumner's demand for Canada, 1868   Volume 46, Pages 33–38

  The Treaty of Washington, 1871

                 Compare Volume 49, Pages 121, 180

    The dispute over the San Juan islands

      The award of the Emperor of Germany

Problems of the United States and Canada—Continued
  American pretensions in the Bering Sea

                                   Volume 46, Pages 46–53

    The acquisition of Alaska   Compare Volume 49, Page 187
    The seal herds
      The American demand for a closed sea
      Canadian interests
        Vancouver
      Blaine's bluster
      Arbitration
        The award to British interests
  Fisheries   Volume 46, Pages 243–248
    Commissions   Compare Volume 49, Pages 159–161, 179–181,
                                    237–238
      Newfoundland   Compare Volume 47, Pages 151–154
    The Hague decision, 1909
  Controversies of the Twentieth Century
    The Alaskan boundary Compare Volume 49, Pages 232–236
    The demise of "annexation"

                       Volume 49, Pages 106–111, 178–183

    Reciprocity
      The refusal of Canada, 1911

                Compare Volume 49, Pages 121–125, 158–159,
                                184–185, 242–252

American Defiance of Great Britain   Volume 46, Chapter VI
  Cleveland's view of the Monroe Doctrine
    The boundary dispute between Venezuela and Great
        Britain   Compare Volume 50, Pages 188–189
      Olney's despatch   Compare Volume 49, Pages 187–229
    Compulsory arbitration
      The award in favor of Great Britain

War with Spain   Volume 46, Chapter VII
  Cuba, thorn in the flesh of Spain and the United States
    Spanish rule
    Native revolts
    American meddling
      Aspirations of the South prior to the Civil War
      Later filibusterers

War with Spain—Continued

        The Virginius affair   Volume 46, Page 119n.

    Weyler's "renconcentrado" camps

      American protests

        The power of the American press

McKinley's Cuban policy

  Cuban freedom

  Spanish friendship

    The liberal government of Sagasta

The wrath of the American people

  DeLome's stupidity

  The destruction of the *Maine*

    The reluctance of McKinley to fight

    Spanish efforts for peace

  Declaration of war by Congress

  Military and naval exploits

    Dewey at Manila Bay   Volume 46, Chapter VIII

      Victory in battle

      His precarious situation

        The blockade of the city

        Approaching Spanish relief

        Actions of the German fleet

          Opinions of the Kaiser

          British onlookers

    The Cuban campaign   "   "   IX

      The American blockading fleet

      The voyage of the Oregon

    Cervera's fighting fleet

      The terror in American shore resorts

      His arrival in Santiago

    Preparation of an American expeditionary force

                             Volume 46, Chapter X

      Hit or miss methods

        Woolens for tropical marches

        Embalmed beef

      The Rough Riders

    The troops in action   "   "   XI

      Las Guasimas

      El Caney and San Juan Hill

War with Spain—Continued
      Cervera's flight
        The destruction of his fleet
      Lessons for the American people
        Alger's failure
        The controversy between Sampson and Schley
    The end   Volume 46, Chapter XII
      The American naval demonstration against Spain
        The recall of Camarra from his voyage against
          Dewey
      The American army in Porto Rico
      The capture of Manila
        Dewey's bombardment
        The assault of the American army
      The terms of peace
        Independence for Cuba
        American retention of the Philippines

The Birth of an American Empire   Volume 46, Chapter XIII
  The possessions
    The annexation of Hawaii
    A new arrangement in Samoa
    The Philippines and the Pacific Islands
    A protectorate over Cuba
      The provisional government of General Wood
      The Platt Amendment
    Porto Rico, an unincorporated territory
  Problems of imperialism
  War with the Filipinos
    The patriot Aguinaldo
      The exploits of Funston
  The American reaction against imperialism
    The campaign of Bryan in 1900
  Forms of government
    The Schurman commission
    The Taft commission
      Civil government under Taft
      A native legislature
    The policy of Wilson

China, The United States, and Japan
  Chinese immigration   Compare Volume 35, Chapter IX
  European friends by the sick-bed of China
                                 Volume 46, Chapter XIV

    The Kaiser's concern
    Russian advances
    British self-protection
    French participation
  The American attitude
    Hay's policy of "The Open Door"
      British support
      Russian evasion
  Chinese resistance
    The Boxer uprising
      The international expedition
    Punishment of China
      American insistence upon Chinese integrity
  The Russo-Japanese war
    American insistence upon recognition of Chinese
      neutrality
    American participation in the peace negotiations
      The Treaty of Portsmouth
                        Compare Volume 47, Pages 171–174
  Issues between the United States and Japan
    The integrity of China   Volume 46, Chapter XIV
      Japanese immigration into American territories
                        Compare Volume 47, Pages 157–163
                        Compare Volume 35, Pages 203–207
      The Root-Takahira agreement
        Conflicting state laws
          The actions of California
      The dollar diplomacy of Knox
      Wilson's policy
      Readjustments
        The Treaty, 1911
        The California land act, 1913
        The Chinese revolution
        The Japanese seizure of Kiao-Chau, 1914
        The "Twenty-one Demands," 1915

China, The United States, and Japan—Continued

           The Ishii mission, 1917

           The Peace Conference, 1919

           The Washington Conference, 1921

           The renewal of the "gentlemen's agreement,"
              1923

           The American Immigration law, 1924

           Exclusion of Japanese

Roosevelt and the Monroe Doctrine—The Caribbean Policy

                          Volume 47, Chapters X, XI

                          Volume 46, Chapters XV, XVI

  Venezuelan repudiation of debts

                    Compare Volume 50, Pages 190–194

    The pacific blockade

      Germany, Italy, and Great Britain

    German intentions

      Roosevelt's threat

        Tne German request for American arbitration

    The Drago doctrine

      The remonstrance of South America

        The response of Roosevelt

        An international police power

The Debts of San Domingo.   Compare Volume 50,

                 Pages 108–111, 164–165, 223–225,

                                 234–235

    The inability of its government

      American administration and adjustment

        Responsibility to European creditors

        The model for management of Nicaragua and
          Hayti

  Colombia and the Panama Canal

    American negotiations with Great Britain

      The obstacle of the Clayton-Bulwer Treaty

      Hay's solution

        The Hay-Pauncefote Treaties

    Controversies about routes

      Nicaragua versus Panama

        The rights of De Lesseps

Roosevelt and the Monroe Doctrine—Continued
   Hay's negotiations with Colombia
     The Hay-Herran Treaty
      Rejection by Colombia
   The action of Roosevelt
                  Compare Volume 50, Pages 185–187
   "Various revolutionary movements"
     The proper selection of one
      The rôle of Bunau-Varilla
     The prompt arrival of the American fleet
     Immediate recognition of the Republic of Panama
      The Canal Treaty

Pan-Americanism and the Mexican Imbroglio
                  Volume 46, Pages 271–277
  Hispanic American restiveness under the leadership of
    the United States
            Compare Volume 50, Chapters X, XI, XII
   Desires of the "A B C powers"
    Argentine, Brazil, Chili
  Suspicions of American friendship
  Futile Pan-American Congresses
American relations with Mexico
  The conference of Taft and Diaz, 1910
  Madero's revolution
    The uprising of Huerta
     The counter-revolt of Carranza
    Wilson's refusal to recognize Huerta
                  Volume 48, Pages 86–89
     The landing at Vera Cruz
     The flight of Huerta
    Mediation by the A B C powers
     American recognition of Carranza
  Villa's attack upon the United States
    Pershing's punitive expedition
     The protests of Carranza
      The affair at Carrizal
  Wilson's refusal to chastise Mexico
    The eve of the war with Germany

International Relationships Prior to the World War
   The Algeciras Conference, 1905   Volume 47, Pages 175–176
     The participation of the United States
                            Volume 48, Page 34
      American influence on the side of France
      Discomfiture of Germany
   The Hague Tribunal   Volume 46, Chapter XVII
   General arbitration treaties
    Root and Bryan
   International agreements

America and the European Conflict
   The American President   Volume 48, Chapter I
    The personality of Wilson
   The rights of neutrals
    The American tradition of isolation
     Indifference and peace
   The effect of the outbreak of war in Europe
    Divided American opinion
     Initial uncertainties
      Roosevelt's opinion in September, 1914
                  Compare Volume 47, Chapter XVI
    Wilson's pacifist inclinations
     The possibility of mediation
  American commerce in jeopardy
   British search and seizure
   The munitions trade
   German danger zones
    The submarine   Volume 48, Chapter III
     The destruction of American lives and property
      The *Lusitania*
  Wilsonian delay
   The battle of notes with Germany
    Wilson's success
     The *Sussex* pledge
   The slow awakening of America
    Armed merchantmen
     Bryan's position
    The wave of materialism

America and the European Conflict—Continued
        War millionaires
        The craze for luxury
      The personal element
      Dislike of Wilson
    Western pacificism
The German campaign in America   Volume 48, Chapter **IV**
    Propaganda
      The German-American press
      Pacificist societies
      Ford's "Peace Ship"
    Secret intrigue
      The activities of von Papen and Boy-Ed
      Bernstorff and Albert
    Plots, explosions, and strikes
    The effect upon American convictions
      Anger toward Germany
      Growing demand for preparedness
        The National Security League
        General Wood and the Plattsburg idea
          The conversion of Wilson
            The speech-making tour in pro-German and
               pacifist centers
      American military unreadiness revealed
      The Mexican imbroglio
        Pershing's ride into Mexico
        The escape of Villa
      The election of 1916
        The unpopularity of Wilson
        His domestic policy
        His pacificism in foreign affairs
      The candidacy of Hughes
        A campaign of criticism
      The pivot state, California
        Republican campaign blunders
          Slights to Progressives

War with Germany   Volume 48, Chapter **V**
    The decision to fight

War with Germany—Continued
    The resolution of Wilson
      The call to fight for the rights of mankind
    Vague German overtures, December 12, 1916
      Wilson's peace note of December 18
        The purposes of the belligerents
        A League of Nations
      "Peace without victory," January 22, 1917
    Germany's withdrawal of the *Sussex* pledge, January 31, 1917
      The break between Germany and America, February 3, 1917
    Unrestricted submarine warfare
      American obstructionists
        The twelve "wilful men"
    The declaration of war, April 6, 1917
Preparation for battle   Volume 48, Chapter VI
    The American General Staff
    The Selective Service Act
      American soldiers for European battlefields
        The desire of Roosevelt
                 Compare Volume 47, Pages 265–270
        General Pershing's expedition
    Equipment and munitions
      Necessary provisions for the future
        Immediate needs met by the Allies
      Machine guns, rifles, and airplanes
    The expansion of the Navy
      Destroyers and transports
    Inevitable governmental centralization
      The Overman Act
The ordeal of battle
    The home front   Volume 48, Chapter VII
      The Council for National Defence
      The War Industries Board
      The Food Administration
      Fuel conservation
      Railroad administration
      The Emergency Fleet Corporation

War with Germany—Continued
    The War Trade Board
    The War Labor Board
      The Labor Policies Board
    Liberty Loan drives
    The Committee on Public Information
    Wall Street and war   Volume 41, Chapter IX
      Morgan, Ryan, and Schwab
   The fighting front   Volume 48, Chapter VIII
    The part of the Navy
      Convoys for troopships
      Prowlers on submarine trails
      The battle fleet in the North Sea
      The mine barrage off Scotland
    Doughboys in France
      The Service of Supply
      Amalgamation with Allied divisions
        Seicheprey
        Cantigny
        Château-Thierry
        Belleau Wood
        Soissons to the Vesle river
   An American drive
    The St. Mihiel Salient
      The moral influence of the American victory
   The Americans in the Argonne
    Sedan, the key to the German position in France
      Destruction of the German lines of defense
   The German plea for a truce
    The Armistice, November 11, 1918

The Peace Conference
   Post-armistice problems   Volume 48, Chapter IX
    Wilsonian justice
      The distinction between German people and government
      Application of the Fourteen Points
        Concern for small nations
        The principle of self-restraint

The Peace Conference—Continued
    Recalcitrant partisans
      The opposition of Wilson's fellow Americans
    The Wilsonian peace commission
      Wilson in person to Paris
      Roosevelt's outburst
  Special pleaders at Paris   Volume 48, Chapter X
    Rivals for Wilson's favor
      The effect of delay
    Experts and diplomats
      The influence of American reports
      "The Inquiry"
  The Conference and executive councils
    The Council of Ten
      Contrasting personalities
      The succession of witnesses and claimants
      The delegation of details to special commissions
        The League of Nations
        Boundaries
        Reparations
    The "Big Four"
      The board of review
      Reports of the commissions   Volume 48, Chapter XI
The League of Nations
  The menace of national self-interest
    The aggression of the victors
    The conflicting claims of small nations
  The need for justice and reconciliation
    The means
    An international understanding
  The idea of immediate preliminary terms of peace
    The lost opportunity
  Wilson's victory over Clemenceau
    Preference for a league rather than alliances
    Tacit understanding with the British
  The covenant
    Provisions
      Council and assembly
      Article X

The Peace Conference—Continued
 The failure of Wilson's advocacy in America
  The effect on Europe
 Annexations and indemnities
 French aspirations in the Saar valley
 The Rhineland
  Armies of occupation
 Reparations
  The blank check
   German signatures
 The tri-partite alliance
  The defence of France against unprovoked attack

The Treaty of Versailles   Volume 48, Chapter XII
 The basis, the League of Nations
 Allied obligations to Italy
  The secret Treaty of London, 1915
   The promise of Austrian provinces
  American opposition
   The rights of Jugo-Slavia
   Justice for Austria
  Italian desire for Fiume
   The resistance of Wilson
   The political maneuvers of Orlando
 Japanese claims
  Racial equality
  Inheritance of German leases
   Shantung
  The American opposition
   Withdrawal of resistance
    Japanese promises to retire from Shantung
 German protests
  Economic clauses
  Reparations
  The Saar and Poland
   Wilson's refusal to soften the terms to win German
    signatures
  German acceptance under pressure
   A peace of hatred and distrust

The Treaty of Versailles—Continued
    Defiant German delegates
  Weaknesses and flaws
   Unsatisfied claims
   Conflicting interests
   Economic mistakes
   Territorial disputes
 The struggle for ratification by the American Senate
           Volume 48, Chapter XIII

  Republican opposition
   The tradition of American isolation
   Personal dislike of Wilson
    Reservations and interpretations
  Wilsonian temperament
   The manner of the schoolmaster
   Reliance upon public opinion
    His speaking tour
     His illness
   The failure of co-operation with mild Republicans
  British overtures
   The published letter of Viscount Grey
   Wilsonian insistence upon Article X
    The refusal of the Senate to ratify the treaty
  The tragedy   Volume 48, Chapter XIV
   Wilson's opportunity for international service
    Partial success in Europe
   Rejection by his own people

CHAPTER XXI

OUR NEIGHBORS

IT is a curious fact that the American people, during most of their history, have been peculiarly ignorant of the affairs of their nearest neighbors. The citizen of the United States has usually been too much engrossed in the problems of his own country to pay much attention to Canada or Hispanic America. It is true that many Americans have hoped that Canada might one day become a part of the Union. They were quick to assume that Canadians of the Nineteenth Century chafed under the British yoke as Americans of the Eighteenth had done. For this reason, they generally misunderstood the rebellion of 1837. During the early years of the Twentieth Century, the American people finally gave up the thought of annexation. The formal end of this phase of "Manifest Destiny" came when Mr. Harding, the first American president to visit Canada,

announced to the citizens of British Columbia that the United States did not look forward to the ultimate incorporation of the Canadian dominion into its own national territory. But with this persistent desire for annexation, Americans have never actively interested themselves in Canadian affairs and are quite ignorant of Canadian history.

Beginning at the time of the American Revolution, a civilization very like that of the United States has developed north of the international boundary. Yet it has significant differences. Nowhere in America can be found a culture similar to that of the French Canadians. English speaking Canadians show a marked British influence. During the century and a half of their history, they have spread their settlements over a vast area stretching from ocean to ocean. With the exception of Newfoundland, they have united their local governments into a closely knit federation. They have developed a national sentiment, not incompatible with loyalty to the British Crown, which has come to definite expression as a result of the World War. The appearance of a Canadian representative at Washington is indicative that the United States must reckon with a new power on the north.

South of the Rio Grande the situation is very different. Spain and Portugal, in one instance, have left their stamp on Central and South America. In most cases, the native Indians were not driven off, as in the English settlements to the north, but were held as a subject race. Latin-American populations, consequently, show a three-fold character: a small group descended from pure European stock, a larger number of Indian blood, and those who derive their heritage from both races. By this population a civilization has been built up which contrasts noticeably with the American and which the American citizen has seldom fully understood.

Yet toward its southern neighbors the United States has assumed from the beginning an attitude of particular concern. The Monroe Doctrine declared to the world that the United States considered itself the guardian of its fellow republics against encroachment by foreign powers. Hispanic America enjoyed the protection but never forgot that the self-appointed guardian considered also that its own interests were paramount. In spite of this protection and in spite of a common language and tradition, Spanish America has broken into jagged fragments that have defied the

efforts of its great leaders to bring them together into a confederation. All too frequently the governments of Latin-American states, though republican in form, have been but a succession of military dictators. Out of a century of political confusion four states, Argentine, Chile, Brazil, and Mexico, have risen to predominance and to world importance. Notwithstanding hostile interpretations of American motives, Pan-Americanism is an ideal that seeks for greater co-operation and better understanding not only among the southern republics but between them and the American nation to the north.

The Dominion of Canada
  The determination of a separate existence

Volume 49, Chapter I

    The Peace of Paris, 1763
      British governors and French subjects
      Acadia, Quebec, and Hudson's Bay
    The attempt to cast the Canadians in an English mold
      Adverse opinions of Murray and Carleton
        Abandonment of the policy
          The effect of the American Revolution
    The influx of Loyalists from the Revolutionary states
      Participation in Canadian affairs
    The tide of democracy
      The constitutional act of 1791
      The policy of William Grenville
      Growing diversities
        Discordant religious denominations
        The appearances of "late loyalists"
          Settlers from the United States

The Dominion of Canada—Continued

 Social distinctions
  Aristocratic antipathies
 Racial division
  The increasing political consciousness of the
   French inhabitants
Rivalry with the Spanish, Russians, and Americans
 for the Pacific Coast
The effect of the War of 1812
A sense of Canadian unity
 Resistance to American aggression
The neutrality of the Great Lakes
Self-government and confederation Volume 49, Chapter II
 The flood of immigration
 Americans
 Britishers
  Selkirk's Scotchmen
   The Red River tragedy
Pioneer life
 Farmers and lumber-jacks
 The development of transportation
 Currency and banking
 Social recreations
 Education
  The American textbook
The constitutional struggle
 The problem: reconciliation of democracy and
  empire
 The changing British conception of empire
 The struggle in upper Canada
  The Family Compact
   A backwoods aristocracy
   Church and King
  The motley opposition: the "Reformers"
   Methodists and Presbyterians
   Lands reserved for Anglican enjoyment
   The disabilities of immigrants
  The fight for responsible government
 The conflict in Lower Canada

The Dominion of Canada—Continued

    The controlling clique

    The opposition

        The French majority

    The question of reuniting the Canadas

        Creation of an English majority in the united province

    The rebellion of 1837

    Border warfare

        American participation

    Failure

    Lord Durham's investigation

    The famous *Report*

The doom of the old order

The experiment of responsible government

                Volume 49, Chapter III

    The union of Canada, 1841

    Futile resistance by the governors to responsible party government

        The alliance of the Reformers and the French

    Lord Elgin's concession

    Reaction of the commercial classes against the British concessions to the French and Reformers

    The meaning of free-trade for them

        Disadvantage in American markets

        Bankruptcy

    Talk of annexation to the United States

        Dispelled by the Reciprocity Treaty

The constitutional struggle in the eastern provinces

The oligarchies of Nova Scotia and New Brunswick

    Privileges of the Anglican church

The land question in Prince Edward Island

    Victories for responsible government

Relations with the United States

Rivalry in railroad building

Closer relations

    Boundary settlements

    Trade: products of farm, forest, mine, and fishery

    Negotiations for reciprocity

The Dominion of Canada—Continued
>> The treaty of 1855
> The attitude of Canada during the American Civil War
> Sympathies with the North
> Angry bickering as a result of British recognition of the South
>> The possibility of Canada becoming a battle-field
> Revival of preference for the Northern cause
>> The Emancipation Proclamation
> Abrogation of the reciprocity treaty, 1865
> American connivance in the Fenian raids of 1866 and 1870
Confederation
> Impelling factors
>> Common dangers from American aggression
>> A growing British desire for consolidation
>> The pressure of partisan deadlocks
> The leadership of Macdonald
> The program of Liberalism
>> Municipal government
>> Popular education
>> Separation of church and state
> The lesson of the strife between Canada West and East
> Possibility of relegating local affairs to local legislatures
> The coalition cabinet of Canada, 1864
> The negotiations of 1864
> The series of banquets
> Sixteen working days at Quebec
>> Delegates from Canada, Nova Scotia, New Brunswick, Prince Edward Island, and Newfoundland
> The terms of union
>> The storm of opposition in the provinces by the sea
>> The refusal of Newfoundland
> The British North America Act

The Dominion of Canada—Continued
  The Dominion of Canada, 1867
 Expansion from sea to sea
  Obstacles on the way to nationhood

Volume 49, Chapter IV

   The machinery of government
    The capital at Ottawa
    Provincial governments in Ontario and Quebec
    The need of an opposition
   The inclusion of Prince Edward Island
    Absentee landlords
    Railroads
   The retention of Nova Scotia
    Local interests
   The lack of communications
    The need of railroads
     The Intercolonial Railway
      Halifax to the Detroit River
   The settlement of the western territory
    Purchase from the Hudson's Bay Company
    Objections of the inhabitants
     Riel's Rebellion in the Red River Valley, 1867
    The march to the Pacific
     Trading posts
     Vancouver
    British Columbia, 1866
     The bargain with Canada
      Completion of the transcontinental railroad
     Entrance into the Confederation, 1871
   Recurrent troubles with the United States
    The fisheries problem
    Trading privileges
     The protectionist feeling of the United States
   The overturn of ministries
    The break up of the coalition
     MacKenzie and the Liberals
     The disgrace of Macdonald

The Dominion of Canada—Continued
>   The Pacific Scandal
>   The Liberal ministry of MacKenzie, 1873
>   The depression of 1873
>   The return to power of Macdonald, 1878
>   The popularity of protection
>   Retaliation against the United States
>   Work upon the Pacific Railroad
>   The contract with the J. J. Hill interests
>   Constitutional struggles
>   Provincial rights
>   Racial feuds
>   The second Riel Rebellion in Saskatchewan,
>   1885
>   The execution of Riel
>   The bitterness of his fellow French Cana-
>   dians
>   The hatreds of Orangemen and Catholics
>   Four alternatives to nationhood
>   Annexation to the United States
>   The agitation of 1889
>   Commercial union with the United States
>   Unrestricted trade
>   Renewed discussion of reciprocity
>   A return to "imperial federation"
>   Closer connection with Great Britain
>   Preferential trade and protection
>   Alliance with Great Britain
>   Equality in the Empire
>   A partnership between colony and mother
>   country
>   The way toward a British Commonwealth
>   of Nations
>   Commercial stagnation and political distraction
>   in the nineties
> Problems of the Twentieth Century   Volume 49, Chapter V
>   The Liberal ministry of Laurier
>   Religion and Manitoba schools
>   Immigration

The Dominion of Canada—Continued
    The work of Sifton
    Settlers from Great Britain and the United
      States
    Peoples from eastern and southern Europe
  Land and railway policies
    Free homesteads
    New transcontinentals
  Laurier and imperial co-operation
    The Diamond Jubilee
      The Colonial Conference
    Participation in the Boer War
    Imperial Conferences
      Laurier, Chamberlain, and Churchill
      Tariffs, preferences, and imperial defense
      The principle of Home Rule
    The question of a Canadian Navy
      The election of Borden
  Relations with the United States
    The Venezuelan affair
    The Spanish-American war
    The Joint High Commission, 1898
      Bonding privileges at the border
      Alien labor laws
      The neutrality of the Great Lakes
      Reciprocity suggested
    The Alaskan boundary
      Lord Alverstone's decision
    The northeastern fisheries question
      The decision by the Hague Court, 1909
    The Boundary Waters Treaty
      Permanent Joint High Commission
        Individual hearings directly before the
        Commission
    Protection versus reciprocity
      Taft's overtures to Canada
        The Albany conference
      Taft's reciprocity proposals
        Rejected by Canada

The Dominion of Canada—Continued
  European relations
    Tariff agreements with France, Belgium, Netherlands, Italy
    A trade war with Germany
    A truce in 1910
  Contacts with the Orient
    Chinese and Hindu immigration
  The World War
    Canadian support of the mother country
    An army of volunteers
      The Military Service Act, 1917
      The opposition of Quebec to conscription
    The home front
      Industry and finance
    The Imperial Conference of 1917
      Meetings of the War Cabinet
      The equality of the Dominions in a British Commonwealth of Nations
    Participation in the League of Nations

Hispanic America
  The stamp of Spain and Portugal   Volume 50, Chapter **I**
    The fusion of races: Spaniard, Creole, Indian
      The dominance of the Europeans
    The absence of a middle class
    The planter, ranchman, mine owner
      Peonage for the natives
    Commerce with Spain and Portugal
    The power of the Church
    Autocratic government
      The instinct for politics
  The permeation of revolutionary ideas Volume 50, Chapter **II**
    Effects of the American and French examples
    The pioneer work of Miranda
      British sympathies
    The effect of a Napoleonic ruler in Spain
      Opposition in America
    The spread of revolt

256 THE YALE COURSE OF HOME STUDY

Hispanic America—Continued
    From La Plata to Mexico
    The House of Braganza in Brazil
  The struggle for independence   Volume 50, Chapter III
    Francia in Paraguay
    San Martin in Argentine, Chile, and Peru
    His lieutenants O'Higgins and Cochrane
  Bolivar in Venezuela, Colombia, Peru, and Bolivia
  The retirement of San Martin in favor of Bolivar
  Iturbide in Mexico
  Prince Pedro in Brazil
Vanishing dreams of confederation   Volume 50, Chapter IV
  The failure of Bolivar
    The Panama Congress
      The position of the United States
    Spreading disaffections
      Bolivar's handiwork in ruins
  Discord in the United Provinces of La Plata
    Rivadavia and Argentine
    The birth of Uruguay
  The abdication of O'Higgins in Chile
  The overthrow of Iturbide in Mexico
  Chaos in Central America
  The departure of Pedro from Brazil
The irony of republicanism   Volume 50, Chapter V
  The procession of dictators
    The experience of Buenos Aires
    Despotism in Paraguay
    Theocracy in Ecuador
    The enlightened despotism of Pedro II in Brazil
    Santa Anna as a Mexican Warwick
      The Spanish invasion
      The Texan revolt
      War with the United States
Foreign encroachments   Volume 50, Chapter VI
  Spanish control of San Domingo
    The effect upon Cuba
  French invasion of Mexico
    The radical government of Juarez

Hispanic America—Continued
   The French pretext
  The rule of Maximilian
   The attitude of the United States
   French troops withdrawn by Napoleon III
    The fate of Maximilian
The emergence of four states   Volume 50, Chapter VII
 Mexico under Diaz
  The contrast with Central America
   Barrios in Guatemala
 Brazil under Fonseca
  Slavery and republicanism
 Argentine
  Expansion into Patagonia
 Chile
  Her neighbors, Peru and Bolivia
   Struggles over the nitrate lands
 Ecuador, Colombia, Venezuela
  Nuñez and Blanco
The standing in the eyes of the world Volume 50, Chapter VIII
 Pan-American Conferences
  The domination of the United States
 The Hague Conferences
  The difference between 1899 and 1907
 The effect of Central American brawls
  Zelaya in Nicaragua
  Mediation by the United States and Mexico
 Cuban struggles for freedom
  The Spanish yoke
  American assistance
  Cuban independence
   American direction
A survey of Latin America   Volume 50, Chapter IX
 Brazil
  The reforms of Salles
 Uruguay
  Batlle and the radicals
 Paraguay
  The arena of gamecocks

Hispanic America—Continued
    Argentine
        Wild speculations
        Political jealousies
        Peace with its neighbors
            The understanding with Chile
    Chile
        The sway of Balmaceda
        Civil war
        The controversy with Peru
            Tacna and Arica
    Bolivia, Peru, Ecuador
        Dubious boundaries
    Colombia
        The revolution of Panama
            American connivance
                The Canal Zone
    Venezuela
        Castro, international nuisance
        Troubles with Great Britain, the United States, Germany, Holland, Italy, France
        The Drago Doctrine
            Roosevelt's retort
    Mexico
        The end of Diaz and peace
            The grievances of the Mexican people
                The idealism of Madero
        Revolution out of hand
            The assassination of Madero
                Huerta
            The new leader Carranza
        The interference of the United States
            The refusal to recognize Huerta
            The embargo on arms
            The occupation of Vera Cruz
        The mediation of the A B C powers
            Failure
            The withdrawal of American troops from Vera Cruz
            Final recognition of Carranza

Hispanic America—Continued

    Pancho Villa, opponent of Carranza
    The third party, Zapata
    The attack on New Mexico
      Pershing's pursuit
      Failure

    Carranza as President   Volume 50, Chapter XI
  Caribbean states
   Central American republics
   American supervision
    Costa Rica
   A protectorate over Nicaragua
  American direction of Cuba
  San Domingo and Hayti
Pan-Americanism   "   " Chapter XII
  Yankee ambitions
  The counterbalance
   The A B C Powers
  The purpose: co-operation
   The obvious leadership of the United States
   Curtailment of the purpose
  The effect of the World War
   Great solidarity
   Persistent differences
    The Hispanic inheritance from Spain and Portugal

CHAPTER XXII

CHRONOLOGY

The Period of Discovery

1000	Vinland discovered by Leif Ericsson.
1275	Marco Polo in China.
1486–1487	Dias' voyage to the Cape of Good Hope; Bartholomew Columbus with him.
1492	Martin Behaim's Globe.
	Columbus' patent (April), first voyage from Palos (August), landfall at Watling Island (October 12), Cuba (October 28), Hayti (December 5).
1497	Cabots discover the mainland of North America.
	DeGama reaches India for Portugal.
1507	On Waldseemüller's suggestion name "America," in honor Amerigo Vespucci, comes into use.
1513	Ponce de Leon's voyage along Florida coast (March–May).
	Balboa crosses the Isthmus of Darien and discovers the Pacific.
1519	Magellan sails from Spain (September 20).
	Cortés enters Mexico (November 8).

1521	Ponce de Leon sails to colonize Florida, and is killed.
	Magellan killed in the Philippines.
	Cortés captures Tenochtitlán (Mexico City).
1522	Magellan's one remaining ship rounds the Cape of Good Hope (April), and arrives at San Lucar (September 7).
1523	Verrazano for France sails along coast of North America.
1527	Pizarro reaches the coast of Peru.
1528	Narvaez in Florida; dies at Galveston Island; Cabez de Vaca takes command.
1534	Cartier's first voyage.
1539–1542	The De Soto expedition across the southeastern part of the present United States.
1541	Coronado searches in Kansas for Quivira (June).
1562–1563	John Hawkins's first voyage with slaves to America; return cargo confiscated in Spain.
1564	René de Laudonnière plants a French settlement (June).
	Fort Caroline on St. John's River, Florida.
1565	Menendez builds a fort at St. Augustine, Florida (September 6).
	French at Fort Carolina massacred by Menendez (September 19).
1566	Spain protests against Hawkins's voyages.
1567	DeGourgues massacres the Spanish garri-

son at St. Mateo avenging the Fort
Caroline men.

1568   Hawkins fights his way out of the Vera
Cruz harbor (September 24).

1576   Martin Frobisher sails for Northwest
Passage.

1577–1580   Francis Drake's voyage around world.

1578   Elizabeth's patent to Sir Humphrey
Gilbert.

1583   Gilbert's voyage to Newfoundland; Gilbert lost.

1584   Raleigh succeeds to Gilbert's charter.

1585   Richard Grenville plants Raleigh's colony
at Roanoke.

1586   Drake destroys St. Augustine and takes
off the Roanoke colony.

1587   Raleigh's second Roanoke colony of
which no trace found in 1590.

1588   Defeat of the Spanish Armada (July 20).

1603   Champlain's first voyage up the St.
Lawrence to Hochelaga.

1604–1605   Champlain and De Monts explore the
coast as far south as Cape Cod.

The Period of Colonization

1606   Charter of London and Plymouth companies.

1607   Settlement of Jamestown.
French colony at Port Royal abandoned.
Establishment of Popham's colony at
mouth of the Kennebec.
Zuñiga, Spanish ambassador in London,
complains of English settlements.

1607–1608   Separatists from Scrooby, England, move
            to Amsterdam.
1608   Quebec settled by Champlain.
1609   Henry Hudson enters Delaware Bay and
            New York harbor and sails up the
            Hudson River.
1612   John Rolfe starts the cultivation of
            tobacco.
1614–1616   John Smith explores and maps New
            England coast.
1620   Charter for the Council of New England.
            Settlement of Plymouth.
1621   Dutch West India Company chartered.
1623   First seigneurial grant in New France.
1624   Charter of Virginia Company withdrawn.
1629   Massachusetts Bay Company charter.
1630   Massachusetts Bay colony established.
            Rensselaerwyck settled.
1632   Charter for Maryland granted second
            Lord Baltimore.
1634   Maryland settled at St. Mary's (March
            27).
1634–1636   Settlement of Connecticut.
1635–1636   Roger Williams driven out of Massa-
            chusetts and settles Providence.
1637   Pequot War.
1638   Hartford Fundamental Orders.
            New Haven colony established.
1639   Saybrook settled.
1643   New England Confederation or United
            Colonies of New England established.
1649   Charles I beheaded.
1660   Restoration of Charles II.

	First Navigation Act, aimed at Dutch carrying trade.
1662	Connecticut charter granted.
1663	The Carolinas chartered.
	Rhode Island Charter granted.
	Staple Act — second Navigation Act: imports for colonies must be trans-shipped from England.
1664	New York surrendered by Dutch to the English.
	New Jersey granted to Berkeley and Carteret by Duke of York.
1669–1670	La Salle's expedition to the Ohio.
1672	Third Navigation Act: Plantation Duty Act.
1673	Joliet and Marquette go down Mississippi from mouth of Wisconsin to mouth of Arkansas.
1675–1676	King Philip's War.
1676	Bacon's rebellion.
1681	Penn gets charter from the Crown for Pennsylvania.
1682	La Salle reaches the mouth of the Mississippi.
1684	Massachusetts charter forfeited.
1686	Andros arrives in Boston as governor general of New England.
1688	New York and New Jersey united with Dominion of New England.
	The Revolution of 1688 in England.
1689	Andros government overthrown in New England.
	Leisler's rebellion in New York (June).

1689–1697	King William's War.
1690	Phips takes Port Royal (May).
	Phips before Quebec (October).
1692	Salem witchcraft craze.
1696	Summarizing Navigation Act.
1697	Peace of Ryswick.
1701	Detroit founded by Cadillac.
1702	The Jerseys united; Crown takes over jurisdiction.
1702–1713	Queen Anne's War (Spanish Succession).
1704	Deerfield raided by Indians and French.
1710	English and Colonial force from Boston captures Port Royal, which becomes Annapolis.
1713	Treaty of Utrecht.
1718	San Antonio, Texas, founded by Spanish.
	New Orleans founded by Bienville.
1720	End of Law's Mississippi Bubble.
1729	The Carolinas become royal colonies.
1732	Georgia granted to Oglethorpe.
1733	Molasses Act.
1739–1748	King George's War (Austrian Succession).
1739–1743	Great Awakening.
1745	Louisbourg surrenders after seven weeks' siege (June 17).
1748	Treaty of Aix-la-Chapelle.
1749	Halifax founded.
	First Ohio Company chartered—Virginians and London merchants.
1754	French build Fort Duquesne (April).
	Washington defeats Jumonville.
	Albany Congress (June); Franklin's *Plan of Union*.
	Battle of Great Meadows (July 3).

1754–1763	French and Indian War.
1755	Braddock's defeat on the Monongahela (July 9).
	Deportation of Acadians (October–December).
1756	Montcalm sent out to command French troops.
	Montcalm captures Oswego (August).
1757	Pitt becomes Secretary of State for War (June).
	Montcalm takes Fort William Henry (August).
1758	Montcalm defeats English under Abercromby at Lake George (July).
	Louisbourg taken (July).
	Fort Duquesne captured (November).
1759	Fall of Quebec after three months' siege (September).
1760	Montreal surrenders (September 8).
1761	James Otis attacks writs of assistance before Massachusetts Supreme Court (February).
	Spain enters the war.
1762	Louisiana secretly transferred to Spain by France (November 3).
1762–1765	Pontiac's conspiracy.
1763	Treaty of Paris (February 10).
	Grenville becomes premier (April).

The Period of the Revolution

1764	Sugar Act.
	Colonies forbidden to issue more paper money.

1765	Stamp Act (March 22).
	Patrick Henry's Resolutions in Virginia (May 30).
	Stamp Act Congress (October).
1766	Declaratory Act (March 7).
	Stamp Act repealed (March 18).
1767	Townshend Acts, taxing paints, paper, glass, tea.
1767–1768	Non-importation agreements.
1768	Troops in Boston (September).
1770	Boston Massacre (March 5).
	Lord North's ministry.
	Withdrawal of Townshend duties except on tea (April).
	James Robertson settles in Tennessee at Watauga.
1771	Regulators defeated at Alamance, North Carolina, by Governor Tryon's troops (May).
1772	*Gaspee* destroyed in Narragansett Bay (June 9).
	Samuel Adams and committees of correspondence.
1773	Boston Tea Party (December 16).
1774	Coercive Acts (Intolerable Acts).
	Quebec Act for government of Canada.
	First Continental Congress (September 5).
	Settlement of Harrodsburg, Kentucky.
1775	Battle of Lexington (April 19).
	Second Continental Congress meets (May 10).
	Battle of Bunker Hill (June 17).
	American Invasion of Canada.

1776	Thomas Paine's *Common Sense*.
	Evacuation of Boston (March 17).
	Congress adopts the Declaration of Independence (July 4).
	Battle of Long Island (August 27).
	Fall of Fort Washington (November 16).
	Washington's retreat across New Jersey (November 20–December 5).
	Battle of Trenton (December 26).
1777	Battle of Princeton (January 3).
	Burgoyne's invasion from Canada.
	Brandywine (September 11).
	Philadelphia taken by British (September 26).
	Battle of Germantown (October 4).
	Burgoyne's surrender (October 17).
1777–1778	Winter at Valley Forge.
1778	Treaty with France (February 6).
	Crown commission sent to America; tea tax repealed; Declaratory Act repealed; Massachusetts charter restored (February 17).
	Battle of Monmouth (June 28).
	Wyoming Valley Massacre (July).
1779	George Rogers Clark takes Vincennes (February).
	Spain joins France against Great Britain April).
	Paul Jones takes the *Serapis* (September 23).
1782	Officers at Newburg petition Congress for pay.
1783	Treaty of Peace.

The Critical Period

1785	Land Ordinance for survey and sale of public lands.
1786	Shays Rebellion (Ends 1787).
	Annapolis Convention.
1787	Constitutional Convention meets (May 14).
	North West Ordinance passed (July 13).
	Convention adopts the Constitution (September 17).
1788	Ratification of the Constitution.
	Separatist movement in the Southwest.

GEORGE WASHINGTON, VIRGINIA, FIRST ADMINISTRATION, 1789–1793.

Vice-president — John Adams.
Election of 1788:

Washington	69	Unanimous
Adams	34	
Jay	9	
Harrison	6	
Rutledge	6	
Hancock	4	
Clinton	2	
Milton	2	
Armstrong	1	
Telfair	1	
Lincoln	1	

1789	Organization of government.
	The Judiciary Act.

Acceptance of Constitution by North Carolina.

Opening of first American factory.

1790   Hamilton's financial measures (completed 1791).

Acceptance of Constitution by Rhode Island.

The first census.

1791   Vermont admitted to the Union.

First ten amendments to the Constitution proclaimed in force.

1792   Kentucky admitted to the Union.

GEORGE WASHINGTON, SECOND ADMINISTRATION, 1793–1797.

Vice-president — John Adams.
Election of 1792:

Washington	132 Unanimous
Adams	77
Clinton	50
Jefferson	4
Burr	1

1793   Genet mission.

Declaration of neutrality.

Invention of cotton gin.

Retirement of Jefferson from the cabinet.

1794   Battle of Fallen Timber.

Whiskey Rebellion.

1795   Retirement of Hamilton from the cabinet.

Treaty of San Lorenzo.

Jay Treaty.

1796   Tennessee admitted to the Union.

Washington's Farewell Address to the Nation.

JOHN ADAMS, MASSACHUSETTS, 1797–1801.

Vice-president — Thomas Jefferson.
Election of 1796:

Adams (Federalist)	71
Jefferson (Democratic-Republican)	68
Pinckney (Federalist)	59
Burr (Democratic-Republican)	30
Adams, S.	15
Ellsworth	11
Clinton	7
Jay	5
Iredell	3
Washington	2
Johnson	2
Henry	2
Pinckney	1

1797	XYZ affair with France.
1798	Naval war with France. Concluded 1800.
	Alien and Sedition Acts.
	Virginia and Kentucky resolutions.
1799	Death of Washington.
	American *Constellation* takes the French *L'Insurgente*.
1800	The convention with France.
	Hamilton breaks with Adams.
	Treaty of San Ildefonso.
1801	John Marshall becomes Chief Justice of Supreme Court.

THOMAS JEFFERSON, VIRGINIA, FIRST ADMINISTRA-
TION, 1801–1805.

	Vice-President — Aaron Burr	
	Election of 1800:	
	Jefferson (Democratic-Republican)	73
	Burr (Democratic-Republican)	73
	Adams (Federalist)	65
	Pinckney (Federalist)	64
	John Jay	1
1801–1805	War with the Barbary pirates.	
1802	Admission of Ohio to the Union.	
1803	Marbury versus Madison.	
	Purchase of Louisiana.	
1804	The impeachment of Justice Chase.	
	The Essex Junto in New England.	
	Twelfth amendment proclaimed.	
	Burr kills Hamilton in a duel.	
1804–1806	Lewis and Clark expedition.	
1805–1806	Pike exploring expedition.	

THOMAS JEFFERSON, SECOND ADMINISTRATION,
1805–1809.

	Vice-president — George Clinton.	
	Election of 1804:	
	Jefferson (Democratic-Republican)	162
	Pinckney (Federalist)	14
1805–1807	*Essex* case.	
1806–1807	Burr's conspiracy.	
1807	Successful test of Fulton's *Clermont* on Hudson.	

1806   Fox's blockade (April 8).
Berlin Decree (November 21).
Non-importation Act (November 25).

1807   First Order in Council (January 7).
Chesapeake-Leopard affair (June 22).
Second Order in Council (November 1).
Milan Decree (December 17).
Embargo (December 21).

1808   Slave trade prohibited (Act of 1807).
Bayonne decree.

1809   Repeal of Embargo and passage of Non-intercourse Act.

JAMES MADISON, VIRGINIA, FIRST ADMINISTRATION,
1809–1813.

Vice-president — George Clinton.
Election of 1809:
    Madison (Democratic-Republican) 122
    Clinton (Democratic-Republican)   6
    Pinckney (Federalist)   47

1810   Macon Bill No. 2.
Madison's proclamation putting West Florida under the jurisdiction of the United States.
Madison's proclamation that French edicts were withdrawn (November 2).
Napoleon's continued seizure of American vessels in French ports.

1811   Expiration of charter of first National Bank.
Introduction of steamboat to Mississippi river trade.

	President-Little Belt affair (May 16).
	Battle of Tippecanoe (November 7).
1812	Admission of Louisiana to the Union.
	Announcement of intention to repeal British orders in council (June 7).
	War declared on Great Britain (June 18).

James Madison, Second Administration, 1813–1817.

	Vice-president — Elbridge Gerry.
	Election of 1812:
	Madison (Democratic-Republican) 128
	Clinton (Democratic-Republican) 89
1812–1815	War of 1812.
1812	Hull's campaign against Fort Malden ends in surrender at Detroit (August).
	Harrison's campaign against Fort Malden.
1813	War in West.
	Harrison defeated at Raisin river (January 22).
	Perry's victory on Lake Erie (September 10).
	British defeated at Thames river (October 5).
	Capture of Mobile bay.
	War in East.
	Wilkinson's campaign against Canada by way of St. Lawrence fails.
1814	War in East.
	Battle of Lundy's Lane — end of invasion of Canada by way of Niagara (July 25).

Battle of Plattsburg — halting of British invasion of New York (September 11).

War in South.

Capture of Washington (August 24).

Abandonment of attack on Baltimore (September 14).

War in West.

Battle of Horseshoe Bend (March 29).

Treaty of peace (December 24).

1815   Adjournment of Hartford Convention (January 5).

Battle of New Orleans (January 8).

1816   Incorporation of Second National Bank.

Tariff of 1816.

Indiana admitted to the Union.

1817   Veto of Bonus Bill.

JAMES MONROE, VIRGINIA, FIRST ADMINISTRATION, 1817–1821.

Vice-president — D. D. Tompkins.

Election of 1816:

Monroe (Democratic-Republican) 183

King (Federalist)   34

1817   Mississippi admitted to the Union.

National Road to Ohio finished.

1818   Trouble with Seminole Indians in Florida.

Establishment of 49th parallel as boundary between United States and Canada.

Beginning of joint occupation of Oregon.

Illinois admitted to the Union.

1819   Purchase of Florida.

McCulloch versus Maryland. The Dartmouth College case.

Alabama admitted to the Union.

1820   Act regarding sales of public land fixing price of $1.25 per acre.

Missouri Compromise.

Maine admitted to the Union.

JAMES MONROE, SECOND ADMINISTRATION, 1821–1825.

Vice-president — D. D. Tompkins.

Election of 1820:

    Monroe (Democratic-Republican)   231

    Adams (Democratic-Republican)   1

1821   Missouri admitted to the Union.

1823   Monroe Doctrine.

1824   Tariff of 1824.

Gibbons versus Ogden.

Defeat of "King Caucus."

JOHN QUINCY ADAMS, MASSACHUSETTS, 1825–1829.

Vice-president — John C. Calhoun.

Election of 1824:

Jackson	99	152,901
Adams	84	114,023
Crawford	41	46,979
Clay	37	47,217

1825   Election of Adams by House of Representatives.

Completion of the Erie Canal.

1826   Death of John Adams and Thomas Jefferson (Both on July 4).

1827   Woolens tariff bill.

1828   Tariff of Abominations.
         South Carolina's *Exposition*.
         Breaking of ground for the B. and O.
         railroad.

ANDREW JACKSON, TENNESSEE, FIRST ADMINISTRA-
         TION, 1829–1833.

         Vice-president — John C. Calhoun.
         Election of 1828:
             Jackson (Anti-Adminis-
                 tration)   178   647,276
             Adams (Administration)83   508,064
1829   Removal of office holders.
         Break between Calhoun and Jackson.
1830   Webster-Hayne Debate (January 21
             26).
         Jackson's "Union" toast (April 13).
         Veto of Maysville road bill.
1831   *Liberator* founded by Garrison.
         First national nominating convention in
             United States, Anti-Masonic party.
1832   First national convention of Democratic
             party adopts two-thirds rule (May
             22).
         Veto by Jackson of bill to recharter Na-
             tional Bank (July 10).
         Tariff of 1832 (July 14).
         Adoption of Ordinance of Nullification by
             South Carolina convention (November
             24).
         Jackson's nullification proclamation (De-
             cember 10).
1833   Compromise of 1833 (March 3).

ANDREW JACKSON, SECOND ADMINISTRATION,
1833–1837.

	Vice-president — Martin Van Buren.		
	Election of 1832:		
	Jackson (Democratic)	219	687,502
	Clay (National Republican)	49	530,189
	Floyd	11	
	Wirt (Anti-Masonic)	7	
1832–1835	Removal of Southern Indians to Indian Territory.		
1833	Removal of deposits.		
1834	Jackson censured by Senate.		
	National debt completely paid off.		
	Invention of reaper by McCormick.		
1835–1836	Texas revolution.		
1836	Passage of act for distribution of surplus.		
	Jackson's specie circular.		
	Passage of "Gag Rule" by House of Representatives.		
	Michigan and Arkansas admitted to the Union.		

MARTIN VAN BUREN, NEW YORK, 1837–1841.

	Vice-president — Richard M. Johnson.		
	Election of 1836:		
	Van Buren (Democratic)	170	762,978
	Harrison (Whig)	73	544,921
	White (Whig)	26	145,396
	Webster (Whig)	14	41,287
	Mangum (Whig)	11	
1837	Panic of 1837.		

1840   Adoption of subtreasury system.
              Cunard Line puts on regular steam
                 packets New York to Liverpool.

WILLIAM HENRY HARRISON, OHIO, MARCH 4, 1841–
                     APRIL 4, 1841.

   JOHN TYLER, VIRGINIA, APRIL 4, 1841–1845.

              Election of 1840:
                 Harrison (Whig)   234   1,275,016
                 Van Buren (Democrat)   60   1,129,102
1841   Death of President Harrison (April 4).
              Struggle between Tyler and the Whig
                 leaders.
              Frustration of the Whig plans.
1842   Tariff of 1842.
              Webster-Ashburton Treaty.
1843   Beginning of the great migration to
                 Oregon.
1844   Caravan of 1,000 persons starts for
                 Oregon.
              Demonstration of telegraph by Morse.
              First process for vulcanizing rubber
                 patented by Goodyear.
              Calhoun appointed Secretary of State
1845   Annexation of Texas.
              Texas and Florida admitted to the Union.
              Government aid to steam ocean naviga-
                 tion.

    JAMES K. POLK, TENNESSEE, 1845–1849.

              Vice-president — George M. Dallas.
              Election of 1844:

	Polk (Democrat)	170	1,337,243
	Clay (Whig)	105	1,299,062
	Birney (Liberty)		62,300

1845   Fremont's reports of his exploring expeditions in the Rocky Mountains.

1845–1847 Famine in Ireland and climax of Irish emigration to America.

1846   Abrogation of British corn laws.

Acquisition of Oregon (July 17).

Iowa admitted to the Union.

1846   Declaration of war against Mexico (May 12).

1846–1848 War with Mexico.

1846   Conquest of California.

General Taylor reaches Victoria, point of farthest advance (December 29).

Wilmot Proviso introduced into Congress.

1847   Battle of Buena Vista (February 23).

General Scott in possession of Mexico City (September 14).

1848   Treaty of Guadalupe-Hidalgo (February 2).

Discovery of gold in California.

Wisconsin admitted to the Union.

First Mormon settlement at Salt Lake City.

ZACHARY TAYLOR, LOUISIANA, MARCH 4, 1849–
JULY 9, 1850.

MILLARD FILLMORE, NEW YORK, JULY 9, 1850–1853.

Election of 1848:

Taylor (Whig)	163	1,360,099

	Cass (Democrat)	127	1,220,544
	Van Buren (Free Soil)		291,263

1849   Suppression of Revolution of 1848 in
            Germany and emigration of political
            exiles to America.

        Gold rush to California.

1850   Death of Calhoun.

        Death of President Taylor.

        Compromise of 1850.

        California admitted to the Union.

        Clayton-Bulwer Treaty.

1851   Enforcement of Fugitive Slave Law stirs
            anti-slavery element in North.

1852   "Uncle Tom's Cabin."

        Death of Clay.

        Death of Webster.

        Origin of "Knowing-Nothing" party.

FRANKLIN PIERCE, NEW HAMPSHIRE, 1853–1857.

        Vice-president — William R. King.

        Election of 1852:

	Pierce (Democrat)	254	1,601,474
	Scott (Whig)	42	1,386,580

1853   Completion of all-rail route from Chicago
            to the Atlantic coast.

        Perry opens the ports of Japan.

        Gadsden Purchase.

1854   Kansas-Nebraska Act.

        Founding of Republican party.

        Ostend Manifesto.

1854–1858 Struggle for Kansas.

1856   Passing of Whig party.

JAMES BUCHANAN, PENNSYLVANIA, 1857–1861.

	Vice-president — John C. Breckenridge.	
	Election of 1856:	
	Buchanan (Democrat) 174	1,838,169
	Fremont (Republican) 114	1,341,264
	Fillmore (Know-Noth-	
	ing) 8	874,534

1857	Panic of 1857.
	Filibustering in Nicaragua.
	Dred Scott decision.
1858	Minnesota admitted to the Union.
	Lincoln-Douglas debates.
1859	Oregon admitted into the Union.
	First oil well, Venango County, Pennsylvania.
	Southern commercial convention, Vicksburg.
	John Brown's raid at Harper's Ferry.
1860	Lincoln's Cooper Union Speech.
	Secession of South Carolina.
	Failure of the Crittenden Compromise.
1861	Kansas admitted to the Union.
	Organization of the Confederate States of America.
	Jefferson Davis elected president of the Confederacy.
	Morrill tariff.

ABRAHAM LINCOLN, ILLINOIS, FIRST ADMINISTRATION, 1861–1865.

Vice-president — Hannibal Hamlin.
Election of 1860:

Lincoln (Republican)   180   1,866,452
Douglas (Democrat,
   Northern)   12   1,376,957
Breckenridge (Democrat,
   Southern)   72   849,781
Bell (Constitutional
   Union)   39   588,879

1861   Attack on Sumter (April 12).

Declaration of blockade (April 19).

Battle of Bull Run (July 21).

Trent affair (November 8).

1862   Surrender of Fort Donelson (February 16).

Battle of *Monitor* and *Merrimac* (March 9).

Battle of Shiloh (April 6–7).

Capture of New Orleans (April 25).

Homestead Act (May 10).

Seven Days' Battles (June 26–July 1).

Second Bull Run (August 29).

Battle of Antietam (September 17).

Battle of Fredericksburg (December 13).

1863   Emancipation Proclamation (January 1).

National Bank Act (February 25).

Battle of Chancellorsville (May 2–4).

West Virginia admitted to the Union (June 19).

Battle of Gettysburg (July 1–3).

Surrender of Vicksburg (July 4).

Draft riots in New York (July 13–16).

Battle of Chickamauga (September 19–20).

Gettysburg Address (November 19).

Battle of Lookout Mountain and Missionary Ridge (November 23–25).

1864   Battles in the Wilderness (May 5–21).

Battle of Cold Harbor (June 3).

Kearsarge and *Alabama* (June 19).

Capture of Mobile bay (August 5).

Capture of Atlanta (September 3).

Battle of Nashville (December 15–16).

Sherman's capture of Savannah (December 20).

Nevada admitted to the Union.

ABRAHAM LINCOLN, SECOND ADMINISTRATION, MARCH 4, 1865–APRIL 15, 1865.

ANDREW JOHNSON, TENNESSEE, APRIL 15, 1865–1869.

			Soldier vote
Election of 1864:			
Lincoln (Republican)	212	2,213,665	116,887
McClellan (Democrat)	21	1,802,237	33,748

1865   Creation of the Freedmen's Bureau (March 3).

Surrender of Lee (April 9).

Assassination of Lincoln (April 14).

Amnesty proclamation (May 29).

Thirteenth amendment to Constitution proclaimed (December 18).

Congress refuses to receive Senators and Representatives from South (December).

1866   Laying of Atlantic cable.

Johnson vetoes Freedmen's Bureau Bill (February 19).

Civil Rights Act passed over Johnson's veto (April 6).

Fourteenth Amendment sent to states for ratification (June 13).

Victory of Radical Republicans in Congressional elections (September, October, November).

1867   Organization of Ku Klux Klan.

Nebraska admitted to the Union (March 1).

Radical Reconstruction Act (March 2).

Tenure of Office Act (March 2).

Overthrow of Maximilian in Mexico.

Purchase of Alaska.

1868   Beginning of negro rule.

President Johnson impeached (February 24).

Johnson acquitted (May 26).

Fourteenth Amendment proclaimed (July 28).

ULYSSES S. GRANT, ILLINOIS, FIRST ADMINISTRATION, 1869–1873.

Vice-president — Schuyler Colfax.

Election of 1868:

Grant (Republican)	214	3,012,833
Seymour (Democrat)	80	2,703,249

1869   Completion of Union Pacific Railroad.

"Black Friday" scandal (September 24).

Knights of Labor founded.

Formal disbanding of Ku Klux Klan.

1870	Failure of San Domingo Treaty.
	Fifteenth Amendment (Negro Suffrage). Proposed 1869.
	First Force Act.
	Organization of Standard Oil Company.
	Franco-Prussian War.
1871	Indian Reservation System.
	Ku Klux Act (Second Force Act).
	Treaty of Washington with Great Britain for settlement of *Alabama* claims by arbitration.
	Overthrow of Tweed Ring in New York.
1872	Amnesty Act.
	Geneva Tribunal award for *Alabama* claims.
	United States gets rights in Pago Pago harbor in Samoan Islands.
	Liberal Republican Movement.
	Credit Mobilier investigation (ends 1873).

Ulysses S. Grant, Second Administration, 1873–1877.

Vice-president — Henry Wilson.

Election of 1872:

Grant (Republican)	286	3,597,132
Greeley	47	2,834,125
(Liberal Republican and Democrat)		

1873	Salary Grab.
	Omission of silver dollar from list of coins ("Crime of '73").
	Panic of 1873.
	Slaughter House Cases (Fourteenth Amendment).

Discovery of silver mines in Nevada.

Virginius Affair with Spain.

1874   Height of Granger Movement.

Railroad rate-war in East; start of pooling agreements.

Democratic majority in Congressional elections. ("Tidal Wave of '74.")

412.5 grains of silver worth less than 100 cents on the market.

Whiskey Ring.

1875   Belknap investigation.

Civil Rights Bill.

Reciprocity Agreement with Hawaii.

1876   Resumption Act.

Sioux Indian War (Custer, Sitting Bull).

Bell Telephone.

Admission of Colorado.

Disputed presidential election.

1877   Electoral Commission reaches decision (March 2).

RUTHERFORD B. HAYES, OHIO, 1877–1881.

Vice-president — William A. Wheeler.

		Rep.	Dem.
Election of 1876:		*Count*	*Count*
Hayes	185	4,033,768	4,036,298
(Republican)			
Tilden	184	4,285,992	4,300,590
(Democrat)			
Cooper		81,737	
(Greenback)			

1877	Withdrawal of troops from the South (End of Reconstruction).
	Railroad and coal strikes.
	Granger Cases (Munn versus Illinois).
1878	Bland-Allison Silver Act.
	First appearance of "Solid South" in Congressional elections.
1879	Resumption of specie payment for greenbacks.
	Arrears of Pension Act.
	Edison invents incandescent electric light.
1880	Start of surplus in Treasury; reappearance of tariff issue.
	Treaty with China.
1880–1884	Development of the electric railway.

JAMES A. GARFIELD, OHIO, MARCH 3–SEPTEMBER 19, 1881.

CHESTER A. ARTHUR, NEW YORK, SEPTEMBER 19, 1881–1885.

Election of 1880:

Garfield (Republican)	214	4,454,416
Hancock (Democrat)	155	4,444,952
Weaver (Greenback)		308,578

1881	Star Route Frauds exposed.
	Resignations of Senators Conkling and Platt.
	Assassination and death of President Garfield (July 2–September 19).
1882	Edmunds Anti-Polygamy Act.
	Chinese Exclusion Act.
	Standard Oil Trust organized.

1883   Pendleton Act (Civil Service Reform).

        Tariff of 1883.

        Civil Rights Cases.

1884   National Bureau of Labor established.

        Mugwump Movement.

GROVER CLEVELAND, NEW YORK, FIRST ADMINIS-
TRATION, 1885–1889.

Vice-president — T. A. Hendricks.

Election of 1884:

Cleveland (Democrat)	219	4,874,986
Blaine (Republican)	182	4,851,981
Butler (Greenback)		175,370
St. John (Prohibition)		150,396

1886   Chicago strikes and Haymarket riot.

        High-water mark of Knights of Labor.

        American Federation of Labor established.

        Santa Clara County Case; Wabash Railroad versus Illinois (Fourteenth Amendment).

1887   Interstate Commerce Act.

        Dawes Indian Land-in-Severalty Act.

        Cleveland's tariff message.

1887–1888   Mills tariff bill debate in Congress.

1888–1889   Samoan crisis; hurricane; establishment of triple condominium.

BENJAMIN HARRISON, INDIANA, 1889–1893.

Vice-president — Levi P. Morton.

Election of 1888:

       Harrison (Republican)   233   5,439,853

Cleveland (Democrat) 168   5,540,329
Fisk (Prohibition)   249,506

1889   Admission of North and South Dakota,
        Montana and Washington to the Union
        Pan-American Conference.
        "Czar" Reed Speaker of the House.

1890   Dependent Pension Bill.
        Sherman Anti-Trust Law.
        Sherman Silver Act.
        McKinley Tariff Act.
        Admission of Idaho and Wyoming to the
        Union.

1891   Forest Reserve Act (Start of Conserva-
        tion Policy).
        Origin of People's or Populist Party.
        Cleveland's Reform Club letter against
        free silver.
        Mafia episode in New Orleans.

1892   Homestead strike.
        Treaty with Great Britain submitting
        Bering Sea claims to arbitration (set-
        tled 1893).
        Valparaiso riot during civil war in Chili.

1893   Revolution in Hawaii; provisional
        "Dole" government.

GROVER CLEVELAND, SECOND ADMINISTRATION,
1893–1897.

Vice-president — Adlai E. Stevenson.
Election of 1892:
    Cleveland (Democrat) 277   5,556,543
    Harrison (Republican) 145   5,175,582
    Weaver (Populist)   22   1,040,886

1893	Cleveland withdraws treaty for annexation of Hawaii from Senate.
	Panic of 1893.
	Repeal of Sherman Silver Purchase Act.
	Chicago "World's Fair."
1894	First sale of bonds for gold (January).
	Wilson-Gorman Tariff Act.
	Coxey's "Army."
	Pullman strike.
	Second sale of bonds for gold (November).
	Publication of Coin's "Financial School."
	Organization of Silver Movement.
1895	Supreme Court declares Income Tax unconstitutional.
	Third sale of bonds for gold. Morgan-Belmont agreement.
	Cleveland's Venezuela message.
	Insurrection starts in Cuba.
1896	Fourth sale of bonds for gold, by popular subscription.
	Utah admitted to the Union.
	Discovery of gold in Klondike region of Alaska.
	Weyler's "Reconcentration Policy" in Cuba.
1897	Agreement to settle Venezuela-Great Britain dispute by arbitration (settled 1899).

WILLIAM McKINLEY, OHIO, FIRST ADMINISTRATION,
1897–1901.

Vice-president — Garret A. Hobart.
Election of 1896:

	McKinley (Republican)	271	7,111,607
	Bryan (Democrat and Populist)	176	6,509,052
	Palmer ("Gold Democrat")		134,645
	Levering (Prohibition)		131,312
1897	Dingley Tariff Act.		
1898	"Grandfather Clause" in Louisiana.		

Spanish American War.

Publication of the De Lome letter (February 9).

Sinking of the *Maine* (February 15).

News that Spain consents to armistice in Cuba (April 10).

McKinley's message to Congress on Cuba (April 11).

Congressional resolutions demanding Spanish withdrawal from Cuba (April 19).

War declared on Spain (April 25).

Dewey's victory at Manila Bay (May 1).

Cervera's fleet in Santiago Harbor (May 19).

Battle of Las Guasimas (June 24).

Battles of El Caney and San Juan (July 1–2).

Navy victory at Santiago (July 3).

Annexation of Hawaii (July 7).

Surrender of Santiago (July 15).

Miles lands in Porto Rico (July 26).

Suspension of hostilities (August 12).

Capture of Manila (August 13).

Peace treaty signed (December 10).

1899   First Hague Conference.

Start of Philippine Insurrection (Lasts till 1902).

1900   Gold Standard Currency Act.

Foraker Act; civil government in Porto Rico.

United States and Germany divide Samoan Islands.

Boxer Rebellion in China; United States participates in allied intervention; Open Door Policy.

WILLIAM McKINLEY, SECOND ADMINISTRATION, MARCH 3–SEPTEMBER 14, 1901.

THEODORE ROOSEVELT, N. Y., FIRST ADMINISTRATION, SEPTEMBER 14, 1901–1905.

Election of 1900:

McKinley (Republican)	292	7,219,525
Bryan (Democrat)	155	6,358,737
Woolley (Prohibition)		209,157
Debs (Socialist Democrat)		94,864
Malloney (Socialist Labor)		33,432

1901   Platt Amendment (Cuba).

Assassination and death of President McKinley (September 6–14).

United States Steel Corporation.

Northern Securities Company.

Hay-Pauncefote Treaty with Great Britain.

1902   Anthracite coal strike.

Newlands Reclamation Act (Conservation).

Withdrawal of United States troops from Cuba.

Decision on canal route through Panama.

Philippine Act; civil government.

Blockade of Venezuela; United States' threat to Germany.

1903   Establishment of Department of Commerce and Labor; Bureau of Corporations.

Elkins Railroad Act.

"Millionaires' Panic."

Settlement of Alaskan boundary dispute with Great Britain by arbitration.

Hay-Herran Treaty with Colombia.

Rejection of treaty by Colombian Senate (August 12).

Revolution in Panama (November 3).

United States recognized Republic of Panama (November 6).

Hay-Bunau-Varilla Treaty with Panama (November 18).

Wright Aeroplane.

1904   Dissolution of Northern Securities Company ordered by Supreme Court.

Completion of Pacific Cable.

San Domingo agreement (treaty signed 1907).

Failure of arbitration treaties with France, Germany, Great Britain due to Senate amendments.

1905   Treaty of Portsmouth (End of Russo-Japanese War).

THEODORE ROOSEVELT, SECOND ADMINISTRATION, 1905–1909.

Vice-president — Charles W. Fairbanks.
Election of 1904:

Roosevelt (Republican)	336	7,628,785
Parker (Democrat)	140	5,084,442
Debs (Socialist)		402,895
Swallow (Prohibition)		258,950
Conegan (Socialist Labor)		33,490

1905   Appearance of Industrial Workers of the World ("I. W. W.").

Investigation of New York Life Insurance companies; Hughes.

1906   Hepburn Railroad Act.

Pure Food Law.

Reoccupation in Cuba (Ends 1909).

United States participates in Algeciras Conference.

Japanese excluded from San Francisco schools.

1907   Second Hague Conference.

Establishment of protectorate over Santo Domingo.

Panic of 1907.

Oklahoma admitted to the Union.

Navy starts round the world (return in 1909).

Gentleman's agreement with Japan.

1908   Conservation conference of governors.

Aldrich-Vreeland Currency Act.

Failure of arbitration treaties due to Senate amendments.

WILLIAM H. TAFT, OHIO, 1909–1913.

Vice-president — James S. Sherman.

Election of 1908:

Taft (Republican)	321	7,678,908
Bryan (Democrat)	162	6,409,104
Debs (Socialist)		420,793
Chafin (Prohibition)		253,840

1909   Payne-Aldrich Tariff.

Ballinger-Pinchot controversy.

Rise of Republican Insurgents.

Taft's Winona Speech.

1910   Mann-Elkins Railroad Act.

Commerce Court.

The fight against Speaker Cannon.

Campaign Fund Act.

Economy and Efficiency Commission.

Roosevelt's Ossawatomie speech ("New Nationalism").

Dynamiting of *Times* Building, Los Angeles.

1911   Madero revolution ousts Diaz in Mexico.

Formation of National Republican Progressive League (La Follette).

Dissolution of Standard Oil and American Tobacco Trusts.

Canada rejects Reciprocity Treaty.

Veto of Underwood tariff bills.

Failure of comprehensive arbitration treaties with France and England due to Senate amendments.

1912   New Mexico and Arizona admitted to the Union.

Alaskan Organic Act.

Panama Tolls Act.

Lawrence strike.

Pujo Committee "Money Trust" investigation.

Roosevelt becomes a candidate for the Presidency.

Split at the Republican Convention (July).

Formation of Progressive Party (August 5).

Chinese revolution; Six Power Loan.

1913   Murder of Madero; Huerta assumes power in Mexico (February).

Sixteenth Amendment (income tax) proclaimed.

WOODROW WILSON, NEW JERSEY, FIRST ADMINISTRATION, 1913–1917.

Vice-president — Thomas R. Marshall.

Election of 1912:

Wilson (Democrat)	435	6,293,019
Roosevelt (Progressive)	88	4,119,507
Taft (Republican)	8	3,484,965
Debs (Socialist)		901,873
Chafin (Prohibition)		207,928
Reimer (Socialist Labor)		29,259

1913   Colorado coal strike.

Underwood Tariff Act.

Federal Reserve Act (Glass-Owen Act).

Newlands Act.

California alien land Act.

Refusal to recognize Huerta.

Seventeenth Amendment (Direct Election of Senators).

1914   Occupation of Vera Cruz (May–November).

Conference of "A B C" powers at Niagara Falls.

Treaty with Nicaragua.

Opening of Panama Canal.

Repeal of Panama Tolls Act.

Assassination of Archduke Ferdinand at Serajevo (June 28).

German invasion of Belgium (August 2).

United States' Proclamation of Neutrality (August 4).

Federal Trade Commission Act.

Clayton Anti-Trust Act.

Smith Farm Loan Act.

1915   Germany proclaims submarine zone (February 4).

Sinking of the *Lusitania* (May 7).

First *Lusitania* note (May 14).

Second *Lusitania* note (June 9).

Resignation of Secretary Bryan.

Third *Lusitania* note (July 21).

Sinking of *Arabic* (August 19).

German apology.

United States recognizes Carranza government.

Villa rebellion.

United States establishes protectorate in Hayti.

Formation of League to Enforce Peace.

1916   Jones Philippine Act.

United States protectorate in Nicaragua.

Villa's Columbus raid (March 10).

Punitive Expedition to Mexico (March–July).

National Guard to Mexican Border.

Sinking of *Sussex* (March 24).

Germany's *Sussex* pledge (May).

National Defense Act.

Council of National Defense.

Three Year Naval Building Program.

Adamson Law.

Purchase of Virgin Islands from Denmark.

German peace overture (December).

1917   German proclamation enlarging submarine zone (January 31).

Diplomatic relations with Germany suspended (February 3).

WOODROW WILSON, SECOND ADMINISTRATION, 1917–1921.

Vice-president — Thomas R. Marshall.

Election of 1916:

Wilson (Democrat)	277	9,129,269
Hughes (Republican)	254	8,547,528
Benson (Socialist)		590,579
Hanly (Prohibition)		221,329

1917   Declaration of War against Germany (April 6).

Selective Service Act (May).

First Division to France; organization of A. E. F. (June).

Food Administration Act (August 10).

Declaration of War against Austria (December 7).

United States takes over railroads (December 26).

1918   The "Fourteen Points" address (January 8).

German drive commences (March 21).

Overman Act (May 20).

Cantigny (May 28).

Start of Foch counter-offensive (July 18).

Organization of First American Army (August 10).

"Man-power Act." Increase in draft provisions (August 31).

Reduction of St. Mihiel Salient (September 12–16).

Start of Meuse-Argonne Offensive (September 26).

Republican majority in Congressional elections (November 3).

Armistice (November 11).

1919 Eighteenth Amendment (Prohibition) proclaimed.

Signing of Versailles Treaty (June 28).

Rejection of Treaty without amendments by Senate (November 19).

Boston police strike.

Steel strike

1920 Nineteenth Amendment (Woman suffrage) proclaimed.

Esch-Cummins Railroad Act.

Harding elected president.